Doubts to Dreams

Releasing Doubts and Learning to Love Through Energy Medicine

Alison Kleppinger

ISBN-13: 978-1987709742
ISBN-10: 1987709748

Dedication

I dedicate this book to my children for teaching me about love. They love me without conditions or judgments. They love me exactly as I am, which taught me to do the same for them.

This book is meant to empower anyone with doubts. I wrote it to raise awareness about energy medicine, Reiki, and our vital right to create our lives. In the book, I changed everyone's names except my own. We all view the world and life events differently. This book comes from my perspective, as my story.

I dedicate this to all the people who don't have love, who feel alone, or abused, or confused by the people and the obstacles in their lives. Love and life force energy are valuable. We all have the capability to inspire and love, rather than judge and cut down. You are important. You have love inside you. You are love. We are all connected in love.

Contents

Prologue: Falling on the Straw   vii

Part One: Growing   xiii

Chapter 1: Something Shiny in Me   1

Chapter 2: A Tearing Feeling in My Chest   10

Chapter 3: Boys Don't Wear Dresses   15

Chapter 4: An Other   20

Chapter 5: Pedal Visions   26

Chapter 6: Feeling It Together   31

Part Two: Launching   35

Chapter 7: Truing   37

Chapter 8: The Ocean Through a Seashell   55

Part Three: Parenting   65

Chapter 9: I Saw It with My Heart   67

Chapter 10: 911   79

Chapter 11: Reduction   89

Chapter 12: A Strange and Ominous Energy   97

Chapter 13: Stupid Stubborn   107

Chapter 14: Sanding Away the Cuts   120

Contents

Part Four: Healing   129

Chapter 15: Their Mere Presence   131

Chapter 16: Shamanic Healings   139

Chapter 17: Reiki   147

Chapter 18: Forgiveness   159

Chapter 19: Magic Green Fairy   168

Part Five: Freedom   181

Chapter 20: Puking in the Bushes   183

Chapter 21: Locks   191

Chapter 22: Connecting with Others   201

Chapter 23: The Tender Middle   207

Chapter 24: Intention   214

Chapter 25: Red Velvet Cape   217

Chapter 26: Cold Ma/Warm Ma   221

Chapter 27: Safe   231

Chapter 28: Twin Shells   239

Chapter 29: Balance   241

Epilogue: Let It Flow   247

Prologue

Falling on the Straw

Falling means moving downward
from a higher to a lower level.

"I would like to have more psychic powers," I said. Jade, my trusted friend, and Shamanic healer-in-training asked, "What does psychic mean to you? How do you define powers?" I focused more closely on what I meant, and said, "Power is strength of spirit or soul." As I lay on the floor, we discussed this more, and my statement evolved into, "I would like to have more spiritual strength." Asking for even more clarity, Jade finally asked the Universe, "Is the statement correct?" I instinctively interrupted her to say, "No, it's not correct yet. I do have more spiritual strength now." I affirmed myself. "I do have spiritual power, present tense."

Jade instructed me to repeat the statement in my mind and then feel the sensations in my body and follow them to any thought that may arise. By now, in my 5th or 6th healing, I paid close attention to every sensation and every thought drifting into my conscience, not to doubt the visions behind my closed eyes. It takes practice and keen awareness. Tightness grew, I had tension on my left, radiating down my side. Jade recognized that my 3rd Chakra (my power chakra) was blocked. My stomach felt relatively stable, solid, unusually so. My usual disposition was nervous, gassy, or weak in the gut.

I quickly dropped forty years into my past. Like falling into a rabbit hole of my imagination, I fell into a hallway of blackness that was partially safe and mine. I saw wide, floorboards passing under my feet, wood beams overhead. I was three years old in my childhood home, with stuffed taxidermy on the dim stony walls, running proudly to show my Dad the black, plastic straw in my mouth, like a cigarette, maybe because my Dad occasionally smoked pipes and cigarettes. Smoking and its risks were grown-up; it represented freedom and being calm and looking cool. I clinched the straw between my little teeth. My sister, Kate ran behind me, my brother, Kurt ahead of me. I ran faster, faster. "Daddy, Daddy, Daddy!" I yelled grinning, my short, chunky legs pumping. I was top-heavy, my straight, brown hair, like a helmet around my head with a halo of sheen. My brother jumped into my Dad's office with one proud leap, but I missed the two steps and landed on the straw, arms outstretched. I saw the brown shag rug between my fingers. Immediate tears. I saw the tops of my hands. Someone scooped me up to a stand. The straw was stuck there, dangling deep inside my throat, above my hanging throat thing. A narrow hole about an inch deep kept the straw dug into me. It was in my way. It was preventing me from crying at first. I was mad that I fell; ruined my whole idea of being cool with a cigarette! I couldn't bear the straw dangling there, so I pulled it out, one-handed. Whew, that's better, I thought. When my Dad checked inside my mouth, he saw the black hole that seemed very deep. Remembering the moment he saw it, he told me with wide eyes, "I stood you up and looked inside your mouth, and theeeennnnn… I crapped myself." My Mom was horrified and worried when we showed her the hole in my mouth. Afraid that I might still bleed to death, although the straw was out and I was not having any symptoms. They called the doctor, to be safe. My parents don't like doctors. I was safe already. I wasn't afraid. Why was there so much worry? Could they not see that I was fine? My mom kept saying, "What if she starts bleeding? What if we can't stop it? What would we do?" I sensed my parents' anxiety and stress, but when they called the doctor, he couldn't sense it. My parents were both such quiet and calm people. He casually told them to meet him in an hour. When we arrived an hour later, with my very deep, black, hole in my throat he was surprised, "Why didn't you TELL ME!!!" he said. "This hole is incredibly close to her jugular!!!" Sitting up high on the doctor's white stool, my knees bent, my mouth as wide as I could open it, the three doctors looked in, taking turns. Lights were in my face, worried expressions, and tasted rubber gloves in my mouth. "There's nothing we can do." They repeated. There's nothing TO BE DONE! I thought. Later, it turned several colors of white puss, then yellow, then green, but I healed. I healed with nothing done to me. No medicine needed. No surgery, no medication, only me.

In the weeks following, on the phone and at family gatherings, my mother told people "She almost died, if the straw had been a centimeter to the left, it would have plunged into her jugular. She could have choked to death on all the blood!!" None of it felt true.

The jugular is many inches behind the throat and soft mouth palate, but I had no idea, at only three years old. I did remember the terror in my parents' eyes and heard the talk afterward of my near-death fall. It explained their anxiety. My brother and sister kept asking me to open my mouth, to show off the colorful pus to friends, to tell the story of possible tragedy, the near miss of the jugular. I began feeling much more afraid of my mortality after that event, recalling more vividly the possible drama rather than the reality of what had happened. Forgetting how quickly and efficiently I healed, I doubted my perspective of the events, and I doubted my confidence in healing, my assuredness.

Jade confirmed it was the correct memory to focus on and follow into the past. "You do have spiritual strength already," she announced. "But my guides also tell me I must remove the block in your 2nd and 3rd energy chakras. There's a belief in you, where you doubt your spiritual strength. Spirit is showing you how little you were when you had the strength to stand on your own, even in the face of fear and danger, you stayed present and calm, despite all the adults around you who were emotionally triggered. They each exaggerated your injury. You were out-numbered. None of those adults had Faith. None of them aligned with you emotionally. You were alone in your perspective," she said. It was as if I had absorbed the trauma into my body and hung on to it, to prevent future injury, or to prevent risks. It was my first lesson in the power of "what ifs…"

Jade put her mouth against her cupped right hand and sucked the doubtful energy out of my belly. The 3rd chakra was open and spinning after Jade's extraction. She removed my doubts in my abilities. I had a tugging in my gut and then warmth. Then Jade said, "I'm filling in the hole in your chakras with goodness and pure love." Deep energy, gurgled and gassy, positive energy moved and expanded. Slowly I came back to my body, healed again. Or was I?

Part 1: Growing

Grow means (of a living thing) to undergo natural development by increasing in size and changing; progress to maturity.

Something Shiny in Me

Shiny means reflecting light,
typically because it is very clean or polished.

I was the baby of a close-knit extended family, with two older siblings. My parents put off getting married until they were older, older for the 1960's. But then, only eight days before their wedding, Jody, my Dad's stepsister, instantly died of a brain aneurysm. She was only twenty years old with no prior symptoms. Jody had planned her wedding very close to my parents' and suddenly, rather than two weddings, they were left attending Jody's funeral instead. My parents went ahead with their own wedding on April 16, 1964, then honeymooned at Niagara Falls. Coincidentally, my Mom also lost her thirteen-year-old cousin to a brain aneurysm a few years later. Despite the sudden losses in their young lives, my parents have been happily married for 54 years. They instilled a belief in me that life is precious and sometimes short.

They were about thirty when I was born. An "oops!" baby, I grew up six and a half years behind my older sister and four and a half behind my brother. I was emotionally closer to both siblings than they were to one another. My dad was a successful TastyKake salesman. My mom was an excellent insurance representative. My main job was school. I loved learning and excelled at it, but being outside in nature was my home.

Visiting with extended family was another big part of my weekly life. Every Sunday we went to my Mom's parents and every Friday we visited my Dad's. My Mom's parents were Robert and Mary. They moved to Quakertown from New Jersey and designed their house just as they dreamed it. A beautiful wooden sign hung below the red maple in the front yard: it read, "The Dunn's", in carved cursive. Grandpop worked as a candy salesman, which may explain why my teeth rotted out by the age of seven. Grandmom worked as a secretary at several different places, including a publishing company. Her hobby was customizing ceramics weekly to share with family members. I still have the ceramic Darth Vader head that blinks colored lights she made for my 9th birthday.

For fun, our family watched black and white home movies of past extended family gatherings. Grandmom smiled all the time and laughed easily. Her hair was blonde and curly, but she often wore wigs of red or brunette. She was barely five feet and stood with her arms folded across her chest holding a short rocks glass in her right hand. Her clothes were fashionable, but not showy. Grandpop wore purple velour and his belly jiggled when he chuckled. He was bald with a ring of gray short hair around the sides and back of his head. They beamed at each other, sweethearts since junior high. Once, when they bickered, he pretended she was hurting him by holding a red tube sock on his hand to fake bloodshed, which made all three of us laugh. Then he slowly brushed his knuckles on her cheek lovingly and they stared close and beamed at each other.

I loved staying with them on weekends and vacationed with them for two weeks every summer, the first week without my parents. Their first born daughter was my mom. A year later they had my aunt Betty. Sixteen years later, they had my uncles, Robert and Alex, also one year apart. "They were like my own kids," my mom said of her younger brothers.

During my mom's lifespan, it was tradition for family to meet every Sunday, 20 or more of them at a time, some arriving from New Jersey or Connecticut. Yet, for me, there was something empty inside among those people. Not my grandparents, but everyone else. They averted their eyes from mine. I scared them on some level. I was different, outspoken, and opinionated. As a kid, I already expressed the notion, "I can do anything you can do better. Anything you can do, I can do too!" Maybe it was because I was a girl, or the youngest, or because I was approaching teenage hood. "I think that guy's a liar!" I'd say about the presidential candidate Ronald Reagan, proud to offer my opinion at the adult table. The grown-ups ignored me—I mean blatantly didn't respond or acknowledge.

Why was it so much easier to talk at school? Why did my teachers listen better than my relatives? Maybe it was because I put my foot in my mouth and repeated the wrong statements in the wrong company. Blurting out, "Mom said she hates the look of bell bottoms. She said they look ridiculous!" No one spoke, eyes down, some relatives in the room were wearing bell bottoms. Oops! No one dared to move. Later, standing next to my great uncle, I still felt ignored, detecting their discomfort. "How's school?" someone asked because it was safe, but then they didn't listen to my answer. Maybe I spoke too much. I noticed they walked away to chase a dog or help set the table. I needed them to validate or compliment me for my thoughts, but they didn't. I liked attention. It pleased me to share my thoughts. They were new to me. Was it better to avoid true conversation than risk honesty or reaction? Why? Focusing on clothes and looks, rather than stimulating conversation, they'd say, "Don't *you* look beautiful today?" They only saw the outside of me. I hated the feeling it gave me when they looked at me, only seeing the outside, my appearance, but not seeing me. "Alison's going to a dance this Friday!" my Mom bragged. I shifted in my seat, dressed up more feminine than I liked. I'd been trained early to hide my true Tomboy personality, trained to make everyone else feel good, but not me. All of them watching me change and grow. It felt more like judging and scrutinizing than admiring or praising.

Admired by my grandparents, I could be myself. They were safe, solid. Grandpop bounced the basketball with me in the laundry room, even when the house was filled with relatives. He stood across the room from me, leaning over with the basketball in his hands, his smiling eyes twinkling. He'd bounce the ball to me in one swift motion. Grandpop saw something shiny in me that I didn't. All my crayon drawings were proudly plastered on their fridge. Grandmom rubbed my back as she talked to her daughter-in-law. She asked me if I needed her to get me a plate of food. I loved their attention on me, their love. It felt pure.

Their house was a split-level they constructed for parties and groups of people. Shrimp cocktail was in the center of the table. This was at a time when seafood was considered special or rare. Grandpop was sharpening knives, while Grandmom set the table. Ham and potatoes with string beans were for dinner. Dessert was a Jello mold with shredded carrots and mandarin oranges. My grandmom loved entertaining. She liked to watch and observe more than participate. Many friendly, adult relatives and friends were sitting around a tiny wooden, dining room table, talking over each other about the weather and automobiles and other people's fashion; no one was listening, but all of them talking. "Looks like a cold front is coming in from the West on Thursday might be a rough week to get the lawn cut," or "I wish the Eagles would win again. They haven't done well this season." My sister was usually sitting downstairs on the sofa with a boyfriend, and my brother connected and bonded with my male cousins in the living room talking about Porsches and baseball.

I faded away outside whenever I could, sometimes missing the happy birthday song. After meals, I usually had one of Grandmom's Rolaids to douse my gut fire. The crowd of people made me feel sick inside, depleted. I preferred pretending alone or getting lost in my thoughts. I didn't like acting like I was someone else to please others. Socializing in crowds felt fake and forced.

The huge rock outside in the woods was my escape location. It was very close to their tiny backyard where my uncles played whiffle ball. The trees were my shelter: safe havens of fairies close by with white flowers on the dogwoods. The lichen on the rocks made for a flat, pale, green pattern of pretend carpeting and living spaces. I liked the sound of the cars driving by. Cracks in the giant rock became stovetops and ovens for cooking crepes and pancakes and fresh breads. I made my own pastries like my mom, in my very own outdoor kitchen, unless the weather kept me inside.

Inside times at my grandparents', I tried sulking, but my

grandpop knelt down next to me on the floor and made a circle with a string in the carpet. He poured out a bag of marbles in the center, and carefully got down on the ground with me. Leaning on his elbows, he was somewhat uncomfortable, but his eyes fixed on me. He talked with me as he took his turn, flicking his thumb, the marble rolling and cracking into the others, ricocheting. I watched his elderly hands in amazement. He caught me staring at his hands once, noticing their difference from mine. "Can you see the old veins on the back of my hand? Sometimes when I move my fingers, I watch them roll around. See?" he said wiggling his fingers in the air to show me. Then I held my hand to compare our hands and I moved my fingers like he did. Then we went back to playing. Each of us took turns flicking large marbles. He knocked his marble into mine and then mine flew out of the circle. I checked his face. He grinned wide at me for winning and he reached out, touched my cheek with the back of his hand, barely brushing my skin with his knuckles.

When I was fortunate enough to have them all to myself, humor and playfulness were a near-constant thread in my interactions with my grandparents. One day, as we crossed the Verrazano Bridge on our way to Sag Harbor, I proudly sat between them in the front seat of the station wagon. The car was packed to the roof with lawn chairs, blankets and suitcases for two weeks' worth of vacation. Their eyes were glued to the white car next to us, a white, stretch limousine. Grandpop said, "That's a really expensive car. See the white boomerang on the back of it?" They pointed to the car as it drove just ahead of us. "That's the antenna for the television they have in the back of the car!" They beamed and educated me, as if to say, 'Wow, how extravagant?'

"We have a television in the back of our car too!" I dryly delivered without missing a beat. My grandparents both began laughing so hard they couldn't speak for a while. During the silence, I wondered why it was so funny. In that moment, I noticed how the two of them looked at each other, their eye contact, their close connection. They touched hands, bent over. Hanging there in that moment of laughter felt peaceful. The laughter seemed like such a long time, longer than I was used to. With tears in her eyes, my grandmom finally formed words and leaned her face close to mine and said, "Alison, you are so smart! Yes, we do have a television in the back of our car too!" Of course, ours was a small, 10 inch, black and white with an antenna; packed away for watching at our cottage, not a color screen for watching as they drove, sitting on leather seats. I was stating the obvious. They loved me, even when I spoke, and it showed. I'll never forget them crying from laughter at my unplanned joke. They retold the story and my statement to everyone over and over.

For every laugh we shared, there were also moments of deep affection. Every morning since I can remember (2 years old), my grandpop brought my grandmom breakfast in bed with a little metal table for her food. Their bed was as high as I was tall. On the nights I slept over, she gave me a Hess's box to eat on, so I could be exactly like her. She kept it under her bed for the nights I was there. I loved the idea of eating food in bed. "Grandpop, your toast tastes the best because the butter melts all the way to the sides!" I told him. I was a spoiled princess. I was giddy. Bringing us hot, buttered toast with jelly and orange juice, like he was a waiter in our own bedroom impressed me. I thought for sure Grandmom *must* be a princess to have such royal treatment every morning. He was tender and loving to her, including when she died of cancer in that very same bed many years later. To have someone care for you that intensely was astounding.

Almost every time I slept over, in the morning, they set me up to draw or color pictures for their fridge. I sat quietly at the kitchen counter that looked out on the living room and dining room. Their big band Jazz or polka music blasted on the record player. I loved the loud music. It was Saturday, and Count Basie Band or other fast, jazz music was filling the living room. In their robes and slippers, my grandparents spontaneously made eye contact without words and linked hands and started dancing to the rhythm, giggling and twirling. They were beautiful and graceful, dancing. They had taken ballroom dancing for years together. I couldn't believe they were dancing in their pajamas!!! My grandmom danced with a dishtowel on her shoulder. I watched wide-eyed from the kitchen counter. Something shifted in the atmosphere, some change I didn't understand, but I liked, a rising, a celebration, a tingling, like laughter. My heart pounded loud in my chest. Seeing them tangled made everything feel easy and joyful. Best of all, they shared their love with me. They showed me unconditional love. They had been a couple since 5th grade and were married more than 50 years. When she died, he tried to follow her weeks later, with his broken heart, but as he lay there in the hospital after his heart attack and angioplasty, surrounded by all of his children and in-laws who loved him dearly, slowly getting closer to leaving, nearing death, he drew back, and decided against it and kept living and loving all of us for many more years.

My grandpop never remarried, outliving his wife by 16 years, thriving solo, joining the senior center, revolving around his family's activities, and his new love of watercolor painting. Even in graduate school my grandpop visited me with my parents several times over my years up in New England. We wrote real letters back and forth in the mail. I love the intimacy of writing letters and exchanging thoughts on paper. He sent me his paintings in hand-made cards, too. My grandmom never lived to see his watercolor paintings, but he became an artist at 70 years old from taking art lessons at the senior center. Each of us received several paintings as he practiced and advanced his craft. They lined my dorm rooms in graduate school. They are displayed in my home today: hummingbirds, chrysanthemums, and landscapes of beautiful flowers and trees. He inspired all of his family with his colorful depictions of nature.

Only a few weeks after his heart attack, at my college graduation, looking skinnier and paler, Grandpop arrived at the occasion. All of us were out in the campus yard, gathering in small circles, posing for photos, hugging, everyone congratulating me. I was dressed in my black, graduation gown. My closest friends and family were there; my brother and sister both came, my niece, Gabrielle, in her stroller, and my parents' friends, Tim and Tammy and my mom's sister, Aunt Betty. When I greeted my grandpop, I wrapped my arms around him and felt extremely grateful. We held on for a longer hug, and I whispered in his ear, "I'm glad you're here." And he immediately whispered back, "Me too." My mom caught the photo of us smiling and hugging. Of all the people there, his presence meant the most.

A Tearing Feeling in My Chest

Tearing means violent or extreme.

Both my mom's and my dad's parents lived in my hometown. Quakertown, Pennsylvania had lovely rolling hills of grass and woods and cornfields, and we walked those hills for hours and hours on sunny summer days. My Aunt Celia (my dad's sister), Uncle Juan, and I loved to slowly walk and talk during the daylight hours and after dinner. Being outside felt cleansing, in the valley where they lived. The land was so soggy, and the crickets were a humming wall of constant sound. I smelled the daisies and the wineberry bushes as we strolled together. We ambled aimlessly, stopping to see nature, stopping to imitate sounds, stopping to create imaginary voices for the creatures we came across. Frogs croaked on the hill near their pond. After our walks, we swung on a wooden bench hung between two trees. The cozy air was magically humid there. Rarely did a car pass on our winding Hickon Road.

"Oooooohhhhhh, how I love my Starlight!!" my Aunt said in a high pitched, sing-songy loud voice at her black Manx cat, with a tuft for a tail and bright yellow eyes. She loved her cats more than anything, and we loved hearing her talk in her loud cat-call singy voice! "HEEEEEEEEERRRRRRE KITTY KITTY KITTY KITTY!!" she boomed, and we all laughed, including her. Many, many cats come from miles because of that cat-call. My Aunt Celia was tall, with long, straight red-hair and freckles on her face, and arms, and when she smiled her enormous grin revealed her kind heart. She was 25 and newly married to a Spanish professor, my uncle, Juan. Celia was a loving, sweet hippie aunt. Receiving any tenderness and warmth was rare and comforting for me, but with Celia, love enveloped me. She was so affectionate and attentive. "What do you think you want to do with your life when you're older?" she inquired. She could always relate. She remembered thoughtfully, "I was always afraid of the dark as a kid, so then my mom let me have a night light. Things in the dark can look different than they do in the daylight." She created a space for me to admit my fears. She listened and wasn't afraid of my words or my thoughts. Nothing was too deep or too personal. Every word, she empathetically responded, keeping good eye contact, as if I was a real person, with real thoughts.

For my birthday, she bought me an art box with mushy round erasers and chalk and different number pencils and a sketch pad. The amount, the texture and the color of the paper filled me with excitement. She sat with me and taught me how to sketch and shade like she learned in her art classes. "Here," she grabbed a paper bag, "first, we crumble up this bag, and then we draw it. See the crinkles and the bends in it," she asked. I loved copying what she drew on her sketch pad. I found sketching gratifying and challenging.

Often in the summer, she drove me to get ice cream. One time, I complained about the flavor. I told her I only liked the sugar cone and not the ice cream. She immediately stopped the car on the side of the road, leaned out the door and knocked the ice cream out of the cone onto the road, then reached into the backseat, and handed me the empty cone. "There," she said, "just like you like it."

On the nights she babysat me, she read book after book with my head in her lap, as I watched her mouth move upside down, changing her voice to each character she portrayed. Her voice captivated me. She read me *The Velveteen Rabbit* several times, and we cried and cried each time she read it, each time the Rabbit felt unlovable. The moment that rabbit became real, we wiped our tears away and moved towards hope. Hope that there was enough love for us like the boy had for the rabbit so that we could uncover our true selves.

Celia looked a lot like my dad's stepfather, Grandpop Deor, whom my dad and Grandmom both referred to as Reds. When my dad was eleven, Reds married my grandmom. A hunter at heart, Reds taught my dad how to be a man, how to hunt for food, and how to provide for a family. Grandpop Deor was super tall and skinny with freckles, and a deep, gravelly voice. His image was stony, but not with me. At the end of our Friday evening visits, he squatted down, his incredibly tall frame, and allowed me to climb on for a piggyback. Whinnying like a horse, he trotted fast across the wood porch and down the steps, we were flying high and laughing hard. I can still feel the height of him and his deep, deep voice reverberating through his horsy-back into my small body.

Grandmom Deor was quiet, short and round. Her glasses were thick, her brown hair curly, and her style modest. Her parents came to the United States from Czechoslovakia and spoke very little

English. I didn't see her extended family much. "Alison, your hair has a perfect halo in it!" she'd say astonished. She bought me colossal underwear and socks for my birthday. She stayed in the kitchen a lot, putting out olives and pickles, pouring coffee, and baking tea biscuits. The familiar smells of baking mixed with mothballs. And when I didn't feel well after meals, she gave me a Tums. Their house looked dark and quiet when family wasn't there. Either the TV was left up too loud, or the antique clocks ticked.

My special moments in that house were with Aunt Celia and Uncle Juan, filled with joy and laughter. Spending time with them meant more 'being me' time for me. We had nowhere special to go and nothing pressuring us. They slept on the pull out sofa. I was on the floor in a sleeping bag. In the dark, I imitated the sounds of my grandpop's hunting beagles outside barking and snorting endlessly in the night. The dogs answered back just like me. My dog imitations made my aunt and uncle hoot, rolling from their elbows and bellies to their backs, feet in the air, laughing until we couldn't catch our breath, sides aching, and eyes wet with tears.

When Aunt Celia got pregnant with a baby, I was 12; they left for Spain quickly after his birth to raise the baby with Juan's parents to assist. I was left behind. My world changed so fast without a conversation. But now it was like every other Friday night, and sadness descended on me without warning while I was sitting in their dining room. It dawned on me emotionally, Juan and Celia weren't there anymore, and I would never be ten again. I wouldn't ever be this Alison again. Trying to avoid my inside sensations, I left the table in a daze, to be alone.

My parents sat calmly in the next room at a roundtable. They were quietly eating Archway cookies and tea biscuits with their black coffee. The wallpaper had white flowers on a dark green background. The kitchen floor was patterned with pink and green squares. My parents' voices were speaking in a low murmur with my grandparents about the news and the number of deer that they saw cross in front of their car on the ride there. The hand-wound clocks ticked as I found my way into my grandparents' walk-in closet stuffed with coats. No matter where I was in that house, I could hear a clock, taunting me.

Sitting in the closet, I remembered what my teacher, Mrs. Graham told us in class. "The only thing in life we can ALWAYS count on.... is change." How I loathed that thought! I rejected it! My strength felt tested. How could I handle this change? I was scared to fly in an airplane to visit Celia, terrified to travel, terrified to fly. Would I ever see them again? I wanted to be alone, in the dark, on my mother's soft, long, brown, leather coat crying, sobbing. I was helpless, resisting change, pushing away the feelings. In the pitch black, cramped closet, the scent of perfumes and colognes, I cried hard. I couldn't catch my breath, it felt like opening, releasing. My whole body was heaving with a rhythm, gasping through the tears. There was a relief in the letting go of it. Holding it in made me tremble inside. This sensation was my first heartbreak, a tearing feeling in my chest, the most loss I'd ever experienced.

Boys Don't Wear Dresses

Wear means to have on one's body or
a part of one's body, decoration or protection.

Back at home, I swiftly moved on from the hurt of Celia leaving. There was little processing or in-depth discussions in my family. To get free from people, I was usually on my bike and in the woods. Sun filtered through the windows as I lay in bed on my back, staring through the depth of my windowsill at the outside blue. I was admiring the tree trunks swaying, branches scraping the sky, and the wind shaking the leaves. Slowly, I sank into the comfort of nature waiting for me, luring me to play. Smelling only fresh air, I started daydreaming of pretending in the woods. The possibilities were new in the morning, fresh. I closed my eyes and imagined creating bike trails and jumping rocks, daring to go farther and higher than usual, proving myself and my abilities. My bike was ready, my plans big.

Most of my big kid-sized plans involved biking down my long driveway to my neighbor Nate's trailer across the street to play. We were full of life, singing, making wooden microphones and mic stands out of sticks. Nate and I sang Cheap Trick's "I want you to want me!" and turned thick branches and rubber bands into guitars. Nate's hippie sister cheered for us and clapped. We strummed like rock stars, our dusty sneakers firmly planted on a stage made of three crates! When we were bored of that, I kicked a soccer ball into the trees to knock down the wooden helicopters and try to catch them in the wind. Other times, I loved playing passing games with a football. I idolized football players or basketball players I watched on TV. Striding wide at 4 foot 5 inches, I approached the basketball hoop, my brother laughing at my silly animations. I slow-motion-dribbled, nodding my head up and down as I said, "KA-REEM.....ABDUL.....JA-BAR!!"

I spent hours and hours pretending I was older with grown-up interests, pretending I had a motorcycle and tons of friends, pretending in my escape world that fed my ego and satisfied my need for adventure and popularity. I called myself John in my "other" world. I had several girls who liked me. My friends and I lit toothpicks with matches to pretend we smoked cigarettes. We pretended we were making out with girls by wrapping our arms around ourselves and rubbing our hands on our backs. Or we made out with stuffed animals. All that pretending helped us cope because we didn't know what was coming and we didn't know who to become.

Growing up, freedom came when I was alone. "I'm going down on the road," I'd yell to my parents as I dove out the door. We lived on a hill, six acres of beautiful forest around us, rocks as big as houses. I rode my bike full speed down a long, long gravel driveway to the road and escaped into the woods. Trees as my cover, wind under my seat, sun on my freckles, I was small but mighty. I could ride a wheelie for several yards on the road, more than my buddies. My hands were callused from my black rubber handlebar grips. The bike became part of me, an extension of my body. Riding on single tracks and over rocks with the pines watching me maneuver my bike, I was handling all of it, powerfully.

One Sunday morning, I leaped out of bed and quickly slipped on my jeans, then jumped into my sneakers to run toward my plans. But my mother was walking up the stairs with a dress in hand, as I walked down. "Get ready for church. We're going in a half hour," she announced. Ugh! My stomach lurched. This was the one day of the week I couldn't sneak away. I was off to play the role of trophy daughter, my mother's youngest girl, girl, girl. It kept me one-dimensional, like paper. My mom adored the frilly, pink and white, itchy, feminine outfits. "It's Sunday. We are all going to dress up for church. And I do mean dress up!" She accentuated the dress because I was already beginning my protest against the damn dress in her hands with my eye-rolling and foot stamping. Fury spread across my chest. I was usually expected to wear a dress for church, but I had forgotten all about church today.

When I was tiny, I was my mother's doll. I easily slipped into tights and frills for her. But when I was three or four, an ugly war started between us. She would quickly put the dress over my head and tug my limp arms through the armholes; I was trapped. It was uncomfortable, lacey, and prickly, so I would roll from side to side, hoping to ruin the dress or rip something. I was desperate to get her to listen. I'd writhe around, feeling the wood floor under my palms, dust flying, and dirt sticking to my skin. Some form of this tantrum went on for years.

And by age ten, I was just not having it!! I tried my hardest to get my way when it came to clothing. Every other day of my life was spent in the woods wearing torn jeans and Dukes of Hazzard T-shirts.

Conforming at school was getting harder too. Showing signs of stress, I spent time after lunch with my head down, because I had an upset stomach. My gut has always been my indicator of anxiety and stuffed down emotions. My friends in elementary school asked me with a giggle, what I wanted to be when I grew up. "A boy," I said, without flinching, frowning at them. In my mind, I was the Tom Sawyer of my neighborhood. I hated church because of the crowds and the smells and the sitting still, but it was worse since I wouldn't feel like myself in that dress.

The one thing I enjoyed about church was hearing my parents sing. I stared at them as they opened their mouths and sang out, "Amazing Grace, how sweet the sound that saved a wretch like me....." I could tell they enjoyed singing. My Dad sang at our house sometimes and whistle a tune, but they rarely made loud noises, particularly in public. This was louder noise out of them then I had ever heard! They grinned at each other as they sang with passion and emotion. Every word sounded harmonious, and I was spellbound. Both of them sang beautifully! But today, the dress ruined it for me. My mom tried to convince me, "All little girls need to look like little girls. You certainly don't want everyone thinking you're a boy, do you?" Face scrunched and eyebrows furrowed, I answered, "I don't care what people THINK!" I didn't know why it was so important to her. She stayed calm for a little longer, "Alison, you will wear this dress, or you will wear a skirt, but all of us have to dress nicely for church. You don't think you can go in your regular clothes to church, do you?" I thought this was an actual question, "Yes, I can! God doesn't care how I dress for church!" I thought that might work, but it didn't. She seemed to be growing angrier. "God made me the way I am!" I added under my breath. My mother made one more daring attempt to get me to do what she wanted, "If you love me, then you will wear this dress! Don't you love me? Do you only care about yourself? Don't you love us? Why don't you care about your family's feelings?" she raised her voice. A felt a ripping in my chest, ringing in my ears, I stood there blinking and aching, but I said nothing. Tears arrived because those choices were too hard for me. I guess I must be selfish.

My mother walked away to get my brother to help her. I admired my brother, Kurt—he was a boy with a boy's body in boy's clothes. Did life get any better than that? He had on simple beige pants and a white shirt.

"Come on, Al." My brother smiled and chucked my arm. "I wish I could wear that nice dress," he lied. "It's beautiful. Just think of how beautiful you'll look for everyone at the church!"

None of this mattered to me. I didn't care what people thought of me, but my family definitely did. "Why don't you wear the dress if it's so great?" I asked him.

"Because boys don't wear dresses," he answered, amused.

"Why? Why? Why do girls hafta wear dresses? I must be a boy too because I don't wear dresses either!" I proclaimed loudly, tears still dripping down my chin.

An Other

An Other is used to refer to a person or
thing that is different or distinct
from one already mentioned or known about.

Luckily, not every morning was Sunday morning. Our cozy house had
woods with deer and birds surrounding an old, stone home. It was the
only place I ever lived. My parents bought it and rebuilt it out of love
and willpower. The living room opens to a large balcony with wrought
iron railings. In the mornings, my Dad sang quite loudly to my Mom
as she came down the stairs, "There she is! Miss America! My ideal!
Miss America! There she is! Fairest of the fair she is!" Mom giggled at
him. He stood at the foot of the stairs, arms outstretched to her, belting
it out. Most Sundays, the smell of eggs and bacon filled the balcony as
I shuffled to the stairs in my socks to descend on the dining room and
kitchen. The two of them glided around from counter to counter, a
working dance from one corner to another. They talked while they
cooked. He grabbed her gently, pressed her body to him. "Kiss me," he
commanded loudly smiling. She pushed her palm into his middle.
"Klep, we have things to do!" She walked to the other side of the
kitchen. He noticed me enter. "Al, come defend your poor Father!" He
knew Mom might listen to me more than him, especially if he had

pissed her off. He often recruited me for help. I often caught the two of them kissing in the kitchen, but not this morning. Today's 'foot in mouth' was when he had told her to "leave him alone" when he was frying eggs the way he wanted rather than the way she suggested. He often spouted words too quickly and too grumpily, by teasing too harshly. I strove to think before speaking, often restraining too many of my words and thoughts. Teasing often turned to sarcasm too fast! I hated running the risk of hurting people's feelings!

Mom went outside to feed the fish in the pond. Dad confided in me once she walked away to do house chores. "Boy, the stupid shit we bicker about!" he chuckled. "Half the time I'm not even sure what the hell we're fighting about!" he laughed again. They were cute together, playful and relatable. To make them laugh, I liked retelling their funny stories. My Mom still cracks up and can't catch her breath if I start her on the story about all the mosquitos attacking Dad. He quickly reached into the cabinet for the insect repellent to protect himself from the mosquitos and grabbed WD-40 instead. Mom was giggling hard as Dad sprayed his face and hands with such gusto, she couldn't get the words out, "That's not mosquito repellent! It's WD-40!" She still laughs so hard at that story, because he was greasing up his face with oil. In his defense, he softly remarked, "I never did squeak again."

After 4 o'clock, Black Velvet, a rare, blended whiskey was usually in my parents' hands. Happy hour on weekends meant they were sitting outside under the evening sky, toasting life. Going out to dinner was usual for them. At night, after returning from restaurants, my parents smelled of alcohol and smoke. Their closest friends and dining mates were Tim and Tammy. Sometimes Tim played his acoustic guitar for me and sang in his smooth, baritone voice. Other times, I overheard Tim saying, "What did the Rabbi say to the Priest?" then giggling and whispering the punchline in Dad's ear. Tammy and my mother were an odd pairing, one quiet, the other one chatty. Together they were gorgeous socialites, beautiful jet-setters and so very charming as a foursome! They were two dashing couples, hair healthy, dark beauties all of them, like in the movies. They said my mom looked like Elizabeth Taylor and my dad looked like Robert Mitchum. They posed for photos often in pairs. Looks and sexuality defined them. Attractiveness, popularity, and beauty were their most coveted traits.

Having a daughter who did not want to pair up with a man was not in their scope of dreams. A line my Dad used when he was teasing with a twinkle in his eye, he said, "First we had a girl, then we had a boy, then we had an Other." Which was me...an Other, a gay, something in between a boy and a girl. I was neither a socialite nor a jet-setter, not one piece of a perfect pair, like them. At 13, that's what I was, an Other. I was queer, meaning not straight, like most people, and not normal. I never heard him use this line until I was an adult, but I understood his meaning. As a teenager, my dad remained very quiet about dating and my sexual preferences. As traditional parents, it was my mom who was expected to discuss the birds and bees with me....the poor thing.

Following suit in Junior High, I tried having boyfriends. I figured, why not try? So when my friend Sean asked me to the movies, I accepted. Then the rumor mill began before we even had the chance for a first date.

"How's Sean?" one of my classmates asked me with big eyes

as we headed down the hallway to class.

"What!?!?" I didn't know her name, but she knew I was dating Sean the day after he asked me to the movies. Ill-prepared and puzzled, I was swept away by my group of peers heading to first period.

That Friday night at his house, we stood hugging in his parents' den, eye to eye, the same height. That evening, his parents were gone. I looked out the window as he stared at me, too close to my face, breathing. I yearned to leave fast. I cracked some bad jokes. He laughed anyway. When it started to rain outside, I said, "Let's go watch the rain!" and broke away and walked past him, then crossed the threshold to escape. There was something off-putting about testosterone, his muscles, the smell of him.

On the contrary, my friend, Missy, who was 16, sent my body into hot sensations, swelling and sweating with or without physical contact. We would watch a movie, all the while I prayed for her to move closer. Suddenly in some strange maneuver, she swept me to the floor. We were play wrestling, and she gently pinned me down. Softly, we held there, silent, not moving not talking, held. She was testing, asking for intimacy without words. Time flew when we wrestled like that, and soon it was midnight. As I rushed into her cold car, to get home by curfew, the stars dazzling gave me chills. Missy jumped in the driver's seat beside me and quickly slipped her mouth on mine before I realized. It was hot, and her tongue slowly made a circle around the inside of my mouth. She sucked on my bottom lip and then returned to her seat. We both stayed frozen, feeling, floating and then she drove me home.

After secretly dating Missy, for a few months, I announced I was gay to my parents. As early as first grade, was when butterflies danced in my stomach at the sight of my blue-eyed classmate Mary. It was super clear by 13 that I was only "turned on" by other females. "Do you want me to love someone like you love Dad?" I asked my Mom honestly. "Then it has to be a woman," I stated steady. Mom teared up and said, "We love you no matter what." Then she promptly took me to a therapist. Last ditch effort. I only went a few times to see the therapist, when they called her in without me. "Don't tell Grandmom and Grandpop about this…they won't understand it," she said as we sped away from the therapist. "I didn't mean to disappoint you," I mumbled. I hated hurting her. I hated disappointing her. I hated making her cry. It was my fault. I pushed everything way, way down. Guilt fueled me to keep quieter about my feelings. I owed it to my mom <u>not</u> to tell my grandparents, after all, she had asked me not to. I longed to share my news with everyone but instead stopped. Fearing I might hurt people, I stopped revealing my interests in girls, stopped bringing friends over, and stopped telling them my excitement about Missy. Instead, I began silently sneaking around and stuffing my feelings away.

One night after going out with Missy, I closed the door behind me and slid down the door frame, crying, feeling teenage angst and utterly alone. Many evenings, lying in bed, I overheard my sister talking with my parents about boyfriends and every intimate detail of her heterosexual social life. The few times I did share my thoughts and feelings made my parents very uncomfortable. They had blank stares if I bragged about Missy, but leaking my heartfelt thoughts out a little felt good. I waited for validating words from my parents, but no response, nothing. After the silence, they usually changed the subject or just walked away. I wished I was normal. I hoped I could make my parents proud, rather than worried. They seemed afraid of me and for me. My outlet for revealing my fears and my dreams came when hiding in my room, pretending in another world, and writing in my journal. Both Mom and Dad have always been incredibly dedicated to family, but I threw an unexpected wrench in my parents' lives.

Pedal Visions

Vision is the state
of being able to see.

My free time in high school was financed with a wrench. My first job was working at a bike shop. With no prior experience, my friend Mike got me the job. He said they were hoping to hire a female. Riding 'down on the road,' plus building and taking apart my 10-speed made me a promising protégé. My boss, Larry, treated me like an intelligent person, as a capable employee. He gave me responsibilities and eventually let me open and close the bike shop all by myself. At 17, he showed me how to use several different tools. Larry was brilliant and shy and meek, but fair and impartial. He showed me I was talented and teachable. "This is a Dremel," he said, "it's useful for drilling and cutting and sculpting and many other functions with each different attachment." He and I both got excited about the new tools he purchased for his shop. Larry shared all his knowledge about physics and engineering with me. Soft-spoken, skinny, socially subdued, Larry was like me, in need of being heard.

Pedal Visions was located near the railroad tracks. The all-glass front displayed bikes and signs advertising the different brands. I began my job by taking inventory of everything in the store. Each week I'd learn another step in building a bike from scratch. Larry called me to the back of the store and showed me step-by-step directions to changing tires or a standard tune-up or overhauling hubs. I loved the feel of the tools, smooth and steady, their snug fit in my hand. Wrenches, screwdrivers, ratchets, chain whips, etc. I learned about leverage and tension. He taught me how to loosen and tighten bolts and cogs. He taught me that my size didn't matter. Even small people could loosen the tightest bolts with better leverage. I didn't need strength or force. I loved the grease under my nails, my fingerprints highlighted in black lines.

There was a line of different sized bikes called Nishiki on one side of the store and Schwinn on the other. The long fluorescent bulbs filled the ceiling above me. There were smells of tires and grease in the air. A sturdy counter with a pegboard hung on the back wall with each tool outlined in sharpie, so you knew where to return the tool to its proper place. The vice grip was mounted on the end of the workbench. I loved that wooden, chipped, greasy workbench. The sound of the ratchet relaxed me. My world at the bike shop fit me well. My engineer mind ticked away with purpose. I was lost in time, focused, and challenged. I became determined to be an outstanding bike mechanic. "I'm going to be better than anyone at truing wheels" I stated to my father and his best friend, Tim as they watched me work.

Dealing with customers took practice and patience. Shy and helpful, with fear in my throat, I slowly approached the full-grown men holding their $1300 bike, like it was a newborn baby. "May I help you?" I took the risk. "Is there someone here who can help me?" they asked in a high, whiny voice looking behind me frantically on their tiptoes, praying that anyone besides me could help them with their bike. Why a teenage girl? Oh no! It was as though I was invisible or a threat. A feeling I was familiar with, yet resented, just the same.

Why was it so hard to believe I was knowledgeable about bikes? Why couldn't I naturally be handy with tools and building and repairing? Why couldn't I be exceptionally good with my hands? I was 17 years old! I had been bike riding since I was 7! Female humans can learn new skills. Why was that so difficult to believe? Did my doubt make them doubt me?

Another common issue was lifting or handling the bikes. Customers tried to lift the bike or put it on the workstation at the back of the store. I offered several times to take the bike, but many male customers wouldn't let me lift it. "I can take it," they'd say and brush by me. "No, I'll do it," I tried to intervene. Did they think I was weak? Invisible? "I could change the flat myself, but I don't have the time or the tools right now," they said blushing as I wheeled away their pride and joy. Jay, my coworker, stared at his feet, slouched over mumbling. He got bikes handed to him just for being in the store. Male customers marched up to Jay to engage him in questions and ask his advice. "Could you help me find a bike for my daughter?" or "What size tube do I need for this tire?" Many times, I approached the customer first, but they dodged me to get to him. Jay was 17 also. We were in high school together. What was the damn difference? Gender.

As a young woman mechanic, I sought out ways to prove my physical strength, but sometimes I wasn't so sure of myself. On a Saturday, Larry tossed me the keys to his station wagon and told me to bring a repair back to an elderly woman for him. He let me take his car and handle the whole interaction. I was excited and scared at the opportunity because his bike rack was on the roof and both wheels had to be put in the gutters and then appropriately fastened. He never helped me. He was challenging me a little. As I struggled to get the bike on the roof, I scratched my arm and hands on the spokes. The old bike was over 30 pounds. I had to heave it over my head to get it on the rack. Once I did, I was impressed with myself. As I parked next to her house, I was exhilarated with confidence. I clumsily pulled the bike off the rack and rolled it up to her proudly. She was impressed that I brought it to her by myself too.

It's no wonder I had my first fight with the new guy Ben when he started working at Pedal Visions. He was older than me, yet he had much less experience working at a bike shop than I. I had for the first time in my life, seniority over someone else. I had worked there for over a year and finally grew more confident and less shy with customers. As I left for lunch with a friend, Ben asked, "When are you returning?" I brushed him off as I walked out, "When I feel like it." I was feeling cocky with my friend and well-deserved of a break.

Ben seemed quiet when I returned from lunch. When we were alone, he calmly approached me and said, "You know, you could at least address me in a respectful tone when you leave the store. It felt abrupt that you were so rude to me around your friend. I asked a simple question, and you blew me off."

His candor shocked me. Ben was taller than I was and had 30 or 40 pounds on me. Also, he was in his 30s, and I was only18. I got angry and defensive fast.

"What!?!? I didn't say anything rude. I was walking out the door with a friend!! How do you want me to address you? I didn't do anything but leave the store! If you have a problem with my tone, then you should go figure that out!" His need for reassurance and respect left me feeling baffled.

Ben was quiet and calm as he said again, "Alison, you were disrespectful to me. I would have preferred you asked me or discussed with me when to get lunch and how long you were gone."

"No way! I'm not asking permission from you!" I yelled. My voice was loud and strong. Larry heard me hollering and sent Ben home.

Later, Larry said, "You know Alison, the person who raises their voice in an argument is always the one in the wrong." That was bullshit. At 17, I didn't raise my voice unless I was certain I was right. But today, I know being right is only an illusion. Raising my voice showed everyone in the bike shop I was defensive. Getting triggered by anger isn't necessary or helpful. Ben asked me for a simple gesture: respect. All I had to do was try to understand and perhaps offer, "I'm sorry. I didn't intend for you feel that way." Maybe he genuinely felt disrespected, regardless of gender or age. In my head, I carried a different story. Ben kindly asked for the same respect that I craved.

Feeling It Together

Feeling is an appreciative or responsive
awareness or recognition;
to experience a feeling of safety.

Not everyone showed respect for my decisions and choices. "I don't
know why you couldn't come see me lately. I thought you would visit
me. It's like you don't care about me or something." My grandmom
Deor delivered a sentence that guilt-sunk me, as she served soft,
buttery, shortcake and hot coffee one afternoon on Hickon Road. I was
older now, but as the words came out of her mouth, the blow landed
hard in my heart. What was her point? Why was she guilting me? My
life was busy with a full load of college credits and two jobs. I had
been writing letters regularly to my grandmom, keeping in touch with
her. She was lonely and hurt that I hadn't stopped by her house when I
was at my parents. Her house felt like yet another long ride away. "I
don't see why you can't get here more of the time," she insisted. *I'm
here now*; I thought as the clocks ticked. My parents peered over their
coffee cups, their eyes tried to read me, then down at the table to avoid
emotions. They saw the pain in my face. Spoons were clinking on

coffee cups. Silence. Maybe they weren't sure how to help me. It seemed they preferred not to wade too deep into emotions.

My heart burned badly. Furious and trapped, I walked outside to catch my freedom and tears began. Emotions were a wave; I leaned on the stair railings of the porch, stared down the stony driveway, high grass on both sides, my thoughts unhinged. Why am I crying? Where am I going? Should I stay? Should I leave? Why do I bother pleasing people? I didn't feel wanted. I'm too old to be scolded. I can't make everyone happy! My Mom quickly followed me outside because I was noticeably incapable of talking or visiting with my grandmom after her remarks. I kept my back to my mom. She walked across the porch, turned me around, and hugged me. Then we stood on the porch steps talking. "She doesn't mean to hurt you. She's just upset you didn't visit with her last month. It's not your fault. She loves you." Is this what love is? Pain? I stared off and teared up. After a few minutes of me crying, my dad came out too. When he saw I was crying, he searched for comforting words and sadly mumbled, "You have to let it roll off your back." "But she hurts my heart. None of what she said was kind. None of it makes me want to visit her," I whined. They both welled-up through the eyes. The three of us stood there together on the porch steps as I wept. It was touching, that my Mom and Dad cried too, and hugged me. Trying to reason with guilt, the three of us standing in a circle on the stairs, we were feeling it together, whatever *it* was. Eventually, I lightened the tension with, "Well, aren't we the 'life of the party!'" and we all smiled a little. "Can you go back in?" my Dad asked. "Yeah, I can," I said feeling better. We went back inside to visit without mentioning anything. I reentered the house feeling friendlier toward my grandmom. She knew she upset me because we all went outside. After all, I wasn't angry at her, more wounded. I don't think she meant to hurt me. Maybe she meant to tell me how much she enjoyed my visits, how much she loved seeing me.

After I left the house that day, I wrote my gramdmom a long letter explaining that I didn't mean to disappoint her, and in the future, I preferred she invite me over and then understand if I might not be able to get there after my many hours of driving. I asked her to simply say, "I wish you could visit more often. I miss you." Rather than scolding me, maybe she could say how she feels. She respected me, because I was respectful to her. We were much closer after that letter. I gently stood up for myself without fighting or yelling, partly because my parents had validated what I experienced, what I heard, and what I saw. I have a tendency to make excuses for being sensitive, but this time, since my parents shared it with me and joined me in the feeling, I felt loved and supported, grateful to be their daughter.

Part 2: Launching

Launch means to start or set in motion.

Truing

True is an action to bring
(an object, wheel, or other construction)
into the exact shape, alignment, or position required.

College was utterly fun. I lived off campus in an apartment in
Allentown with my high school friend Jane. She was family. We
enjoyed drinking and dancing often. We put in long hours partying,
but remained productive at work and academically. I even got a job as
a bartender my freshman year. Wads of ones filled my pockets by the
time I closed the bar at 2 AM. I enjoyed the responsibility, the cash,
and the independence.

Despite the money I was making, Jane and I ultimately
needed a third roommate for help with rent, which brought Mindy into
our lives. She had recently been released from rehabilitation for
alcoholism. Naturally, she and I quickly became an item. Mindy was
smart and childish and charming—when she was sober. She danced
out of a room backward, bopping her hair side to side and waving her
arms out in front of her up and down, like a sixties dancer. Belly

laughing was usual with Mindy and Jane. But after months, we realized Mindy had begun drinking again. "Did you drink all the coconut rum?" Jane asked, gazing through a clear, empty bottle at me. We questioned Mindy about it. She immediately denied drinking the rum. But she became angry and accusatory when she was drunk. Her witty sense of humor became stupid and sloppy. One time, she got so drunk she wouldn't let me leave the apartment. She stood in front of the door and pushed me away. To get away, I jumped off the second-floor balcony. She was strong and drunk, and I was scared and pissed off. I looked forward to moving away to graduate school.

After a few years, I started attending AA meetings with Mindy and studying the 12 step program. She and I would go to churches to meet with other alcoholics. I learned a lot from those meetings about other people's struggles and codependence. From homemakers to folks who were homeless, alcohol and other drugs took over their lives. The message was clear, addicts needed to surrender and give up trying to have power over the drug of their choice. Meaning; they didn't have a choice, they had to stop ever being around their addictions. There was no happy medium or willpower. It ruled you. It controlled you, not you controlling it. The 12 step program worked for tons of adults who were addicted to something, whether it be food, or alcohol, or exercise, or cocaine. I learned how they incorporated a forgiving "higher power" rather than a religious belief of a God who would punish them. It was inclusive rather than exclusive. I liked the positive image they associated with God. AA members learned to give up their personal beliefs to let a higher power help them recover from their addiction; one day at a time. It was my first experience of how the human condition of self-deprecation can destroy your life and everyone who loves you.

Unfortunately, Mindy didn't learn much from AA. She never worked the steps. Today, I still wonder why I lived with a newly rehabbed alcoholic. Or more importantly, why did I stay with her for all four years of college? Somewhere deep inside, I didn't see the option to kick her out. My needs were not more important than hers. "Who do you think you are?" said my inner voice. I didn't make decisions based on my needs. I made decisions based on hers.

In college, I studied psychology and philosophy. My two favorite classes were "Friendship and Love" and "Existentialism." The professor, who taught philosophy, was also my favorite professor, Father Ryan. He leaned in close with his blue, blue eyes and said, "Is this really a table? Is it truly here? Huh? Prove it! Why, because you see it because you feel it? Debate with me! Start with three reasons the chair is there, and I will refute all three reasons." He was a genius. He had a steady faith in his eyes. He believed in something I had yet to understand. A mystery he called God or Life force energy. He was willing to let me ask questions, then discover my own answers. He gave great hints about something beyond my thoughts and feelings but didn't divulge how my mind created my reality. Truth is debatable, he taught, unless it's rooted in God. So he taught me to question everything, and then to solidify my beliefs and the power of my intentions by debating and understanding both sides. Rather than lecturing his class about truth through the voice of God, he allowed us to find the truth on our own. Father Ryan was sweet and likable and spoke eloquently in front of crowds. In fact, he gave sermons at my local Catholic church, so my family knew him and admired him too. He was a storyteller, a mentor, and most of all, a man of Faith.

Another of my favorite professors was Jill Stein, the athletic administrator of my college. She taught "Women in Sports" and "Events Management." As I strolled past her one day my senior year, she called out to me, "Hey!" Jill was Jewish and new to our college and a gay woman. I liked her confidence, her rebellion, so I entered her small, but organized office with my mind open. "What are your plans for graduate school?" she asked in her strong southern accent. I shrugged. As usual, I had no plan. I glanced at the round glass thing on her desk, the many degrees on her wall, her Ph.D. in Education. She said, "Sit down and tell me what you've been doing. Do you have a resume yet?" I shrugged again. Together, after about an hour, we drafted what looked like a pretty good resume. She wrote everything down as I talked about my life in high school and college thus far. She leaned across her desk and said seriously, "Springfield College was my ticket to any job I wanted.....and it's going to be your ticket too!"

Springfield College did end up being my ticket to Graduate School, and to my initial experience as a coach. About six months later, I was asked to be an assistant coach of volleyball as a graduate assistant at Springfield College. The coaching job paid for my Master's degree tuition, plus a stipend! The coach they initially hired was now pregnant and on maternity leave. I was their next choice!

"You really want me to be the assistant volleyball coach?" I asked the head coach over the phone.

"Yeah! Do you know somebody better?" he joked.

I accepted the graduate position dumbstruck. I hung up and told my Dad I got the coaching job. My graduate degree would be free! He cried at the news and hugged me. I was moving away to Massachusetts. I threw a big party with my closest friends, leaving

Mindy behind.

Leaving home proved a blessing and a curse. The small campus at Springfield College fit me, but I missed my close friends like Jane. Leaving my support system of friends and family was painful but worth it. I cried nightly in my dorm room the first week in Massachusetts. Narrow, cold, cement walls with fluorescent lights. The highlight was that I lived only 30 minutes from Northampton, a town renowned for many lesbian residents. To live in a place where women who loved women outnumbered others was a novel, blissful idea.

I confidently strolled into Northampton Bicycle alone and got another job. I was the first female employee hired there. Quickly, my co-workers and my manager became my closest friends. I enjoyed the area so much I started couch surfing at several friends' homes until I could find an apartment in town and commute to Springfield College. My parents drove up and helped me move into Summer Street, my first basement apartment.

I lived a mile from Northampton Bike and rode my bike to work, particularly in the summers. Back behind the bike workbench, I loved building new bikes. I picked up many hours and had fun joking with my fellow mechanics. One recurring customer was Samantha Sanchez. Her voice, her smile, and all five foot of her were attractive. Dark haired and dark complexion, we resembled each other. She spoke eloquently with a Floridian accent, "What should I buy for rain? What should I do if I get a flat?" I answered her questions and trained her on bike repairs. Standing close to her in the shop, it was like electricity.

She told me she was planning to ride her bike from Massachusetts to Florida, camping all the way until she reached her parents' home in Orlando. I sold her a touring bike, the panniers, the parts, and all the necessities for her month-long trip.

I finally worked up the nerve to call her and ask her out on a date. I left her a bumbling message. "Hi. This is Alison from the bike shop. Maybe we could go out sometime?" I was a dork.

She graciously left me a message on my voicemail that I kept playing over and over again. She sounded nervous too, which made me hopeful. "Um, hi. This is Samantha. Yeah. Hi. I'd be interested in going out sometime, yes. Um…yeah!" She told me later, "I used to refer to you as the 'cute little bike dyke' to my friends." Samantha was athletic, funny, super smart, and kind, whereas I viewed myself as goofy, slow, and socially awkward. My most significant flaw was my anxiety. I clutched it like an excuse note to prevent me from trying new things or risking losses. She was brave to ride her bike alone to Florida. I found it difficult to believe that she liked me at all.

Samantha and I dated for only a few months during my final year of grad school. Eventually, she was fully prepared to go on her camping trip to Florida and left with only a backpack on her bicycle. I bought her crystals for supportive energy. Still, I was scared I would never see her again. I hated goodbyes.

The day before she left, we sat in a local diner at breakfast sipping coffee. She looked up from a long silence and said, "Please promise me that you'll remember that no matter what flaky things I do in the future, I loved you. I mean, I do love you."

"Sure," I responded. But I didn't remember. And I quickly lost all faith in Samantha when she didn't return from Florida and in fact, began searching for jobs there. Everyone, even strangers, said things like, "She's not coming back, you know," and, "You're 23, and she's 20? That's never going to last!"

As people who didn't even matter got in my head about Samantha, my doubts tripled. I started to lose my mind a little without my girlfriend there to reassure me. I sought friends to console me and began partying and drinking too much. Springfield College had a Gay and Lesbian Alliance group (GALA), and I became the treasurer, yet remained private about my sexuality on campus. The new environment of college kids didn't feel open to homosexuals. Many of my volleyball players made derogatory comments such as, "The softball team is a bunch of dykes!" There was an unspoken agreement to just not talk about sexuality at all. Not even the lesbian professors were open about their sexuality. I kept quiet with my head down, afraid to be a target.

Through GALA, I met many long-term friends, including Jackie at a music concert. Jackie spoke honestly, without hesitation. Her gait was self-assured and her eye contact excellent. She noticed me early on. "I knew when I saw you that you were going to change my life," she remembered. I noticed her too. Jackie was a registered nurse working at a great job at a large hospital. She invited me over for dinner and wore low cut blouses. We watched movies in my apartment until late at night. She bought me journals and seashells. When I went to her house, it was dimly lit with candles and soft music played. We took long walks in the newly fallen snow. We talked on the phone for hours and hours. I had trouble refusing her advances because she was attractive, charming, and sweet. I remained honest with Jackie about having a girlfriend and with Samantha about the fact that I had begun dating Jackie.

Acknowledging my physical attraction to Jackie made me

feel weak and irresponsible. Like my lust was more willful than my heart. I was incredibly wobbly about what I wanted, or who I wanted. I wasn't making a decision, so Samantha did. One evening, she called and said, "I may regret this for the rest of my life, but I have to let you go if you want to date Jackie. You deserve to be happy." She felt I dated Jackie too often, so we broke up. The pain of losing Samantha was self-inflicted. Crying, I sunk into suffering like a warm, familiar blanket of grief. I hid away my vulnerable, tender side. My heart was already broken when I met Jackie, but I told myself I could ignore it. Ignore connection. Ignore the need for love. *'Love sucks!'* was my new mantra.

For months, I alternated sleeping between my apartment and Jackie's. I don't remember details during that time, because I was heart-broken. Samantha left me, but I aimed my hurt at preparing to finish graduate school. I diligently rehearsed for my Master's Thesis in Sport Psychology defense presentation that fall. I focused. I sat on the floor of Jackie's apartment with my laptop on her couch memorizing and talking out loud to myself. Practicing helped my self-confidence. My goal was to put all my efforts into creating a good talk. My thesis was about gender differences in goal orientation. My subjects were male and female basketball players. I aimed to find out what motivated athletes. I enjoyed the whole process of research and had a solid background from my undergraduate studies.

The defense went incredibly well!!! During the talk, I was comfortable and confident to the highest degree. Remembering the feeling makes me want to do more presentations. The PowerPoint slides were unique and impressive. I graduated! As I left my talk, students I didn't even know shook my hands and congratulated me.

Each of my advisors told me it was an exceptional defense with dazzling moving bullets. My feet weren't touching the ground when I left that meeting! The feeling after I defended was pure adrenalin. My vision improved, colors vividly popped. Strutting around Northampton, my mind played a slow montage of restaurants that were more appealing, strangers who were friendlier, and the sky appeared bluer. I had a type of awakening, noticing how much of my stress had been a veil between my perceptions and reality. This was the first time I noticed the influential power my moods had on my perceptions; good or bad.

Another significant summer evening, weeks after graduating, Jackie and I ran into the kitchen together for a snack in the dark. Breathing too heavy and giggling, we opened the fridge and whispered as we popped grapes past our lips. Everything slowed as I stared into Jackie's happy face as the dim light of the moon revealed one side of her. I heard these words in my head: *Stay with her. You're a good team. She's reliable and kind and hardworking. She won't ever leave you. She will motivate you to move your life wherever you wish to go.* Jackie viewed me as a hero. Her admiration filled me. She believed in me genuinely, more than I believed in myself. I held on to that. A couple of months later, I moved into her apartment.

At first, our time together was kind and peaceful. We sat in a quiet, sunlit room with soft music and share space. Jackie quietly painted while I wrote poems. She brought me food on bed tables like my grandfather. I made her homemade gnocchi like her grandmother used to make. We learned to make soups together.

Jackie supported me for over a year, while I looked for work in my field. I worked at two different bike shops, plus tutoring some students in the evenings, plus working with mental health clients, and data management for a small company that sold field hockey equipment. All of those jobs added up to $200 per week. All my income went to my car payment and my school loans. With no signs of career prospects after six months, my already forlorn self-esteem plummeted even further. *How would I ever find a job?* I wanted a career to appear, more than money. I ached for purpose in my days. It felt like I was carrying five bowling balls at once, swimming against the river current. Part of me wanted to sprint home to my parents! *Sport Psychology degree, what was I thinking? What had I done?*

"Your degree and a dime will buy you a cup of coffee!" one of the bikers at work joked. He thought a Master's degree in Sport Psychology was useless.

As he said this, I was spinning the wheels on the truing stand, my fingers barely touching the metal, like playing harp. Head bowed, making wheels or music made me feel useful. Eyes fixed, lost in the process, without forethought about the finished product, I was creating. Each of my five fingers was grasping the spokes, pushing them, then tightening and loosening the nipples on the end of each spoke. More tension applied here, less stress applied there, to get the rim to spin centered. The rim pulled in the direction that I added tension. The spokes vanished when you spun the wheel fast enough, blended and balanced. The whole is greater than the sum of its parts. Like life, every small move toward center counted. The more tension added, the stronger the wheel became. I took a deep breath and remembered all that Larry taught me. A spoke in life, I was true.

Jackie supported my job searches. She had faith in my abilities. She knew I would get a job, but I failed to see any hope. I applied for several jobs in the area and eventually had an interview. Finally, I landed my first full-time salaried job as a Clinical Research Assistant at John Dempsey Hospital and commuted an hour through Hartford. In the same day, I found out my excellent new salary, and received a huge tax return. Standing by the mailbox outside, beside our busy road, Jackie and I jumped up and down hugging, then celebrated with a trip to Provincetown. We had the time of our lives there. Hopping in the car that evening, I drove while she looked at maps to guide us to the end of Cape Cod. It only took 3 hours. P-town included sandy beaches and water-side decks and the pumping of bass drums, and same-sex couples. We rented a clean, cozy, sophisticated bed and breakfast from two kind and sweet gay men who talked with their hands. "Have you girls been with us before? We have bikes you can tour around on and kayaks you can borrow! Please make yourselves at home! We love entertaining, so feel free to join us for breakfast in the morning. We'll have French toast and all kinds of yogurt and fruit! You girls come find us if you need anything at all!" Teal and navy blue striped pillows on wicker furniture lined our room. Jackie and I headed out for the tea dance! The tea dance was nightlife dancing and bar music starting at teatime or 4 pm. Many, many lean gay men without shirts in cut-off shorts held hands. Oh, and a few lesbians. The center road (Commercial Street) was for posing, posturing, and people watching.

One evening, after eating fantastic lobster and shrimp at a restaurant, we got so drunk we couldn't remember if we paid when we stumbled back out to Commercial Street holding hands. We strolled around shopping, leaning on each other, touching trinkets, laughing in all the quaint shops. Those times seemed so carefree.

We settled into our lives together for the next few years. Jackie and I enjoyed our summer vacations camping or relaxing in small cottages at York Beach, Maine. We read books all day and grilled great gourmet dishes. When we met, she had an Associate's Degree in nursing, but she was a registered nurse. As we lived and worked together, she went to college for her Bachelor's in nursing and then her Master's degree from the University of Massachusetts. She became a Pediatric Nurse Practitioner. We both enjoyed working and living as grown adults. But year after year, things got worse and worse. Kindness fell away. Weekends meant chores and cleaning for Jackie, so I, of course, joined her against my beliefs that play was critical. To attempt to get my needs met, I asked her to do more outdoor activities with me or find new playful hobbies, but she said, "I like photography. I have my pictures. I don't need anything physically challenging." Slowly some of my athletic hobbies faded away. Resentment replaced them. I realized I was working too much and never played. My journals reflected lists of sports and activities I craved. I wrote down ways to avoid upsetting Jackie. Our fights were more often during her college stress. She said I was "negative and intense" at her. So I tried to change. I needed more activities and exercise. Monthly I attempted to mountain bike with friends, but I wanted to share athletic activities with Jackie. She often resented me for going off to play without her. But she didn't enjoy joining me either. We couldn't find an activity we both enjoyed together.

Two summers after we met, we grabbed the Trek bike I sold her and mine and road around Hadley. I loved it! As we climbed a few hills, we stopped and stared at the views of beautiful, old barns on the tobacco farmlands. As I rounded up another hill, I noticed Jackie got off her bike and started pushing it up to me. I stopped and waited. She was crying and sweating. "Are you trying to kill me? How could you? How could you? You're too far ahead of me, and you're not slowing down!" She began bawling. I didn't think I had gotten too far ahead of her, but she continued to sob as she explained, "You don't realize how much exercise was a punishment in my childhood. My father forced me to exercise even when I didn't want to."

I tried to apologize, but we never biked together again. How could I please Jackie and myself? I wrote in my journals, "Taking care of me means Jackie hates me." It was a double-bind. I couldn't win. I wasn't accustomed to hollering the way she did either. She instantly started reacting without much warning. After I went out with friends, I came home to her sick or in bed with a migraine. The payback for my independence was painful, to the point that I tried to avoid her rage. Reading a book, one time she snatched it from my hands and started pointing in my face, yelling that I had made her react!! It was my fault she was reacting in anger. She said I had been baiting her all day to fight. Was she projecting? Did I bait her? I doubted myself. I didn't think I was baiting at all. Instead, I believed her, because feeling fury at her was better than feeling nothing at all. I craved emotions! Passion had evaporated between us, so I craved affection. I craved her touch, but she didn't want to be physical at all. I craved connection. "I can't be close with you," she said, "not when you don't connect with me." I was completely lost. *How should I connect? Isn't affection and making love connecting?*

We frequently went out for our anniversary dinners at Green Street Café. It was the one special time we made a conscious effort to connect and even tried to make love after. Several times I noticed a trend. As I talked about what we might want to do in our future, Jackie became teary and apologetic.

"I'm sorry I haven't been interested in being intimate lately."

"It's okay, you're just stressed," I said to try and help her.

"But I want you to know I love you. It's been my goal to get in shape and feel sexy again for you, and for us." More tears appeared, streaming faster now.

"I've not felt like myself in my body at all. I hate the way I look!"

"But you're beautiful. I think your body's fine. Maybe we could start exercising more or change how we eat?"

"But it's so much easier for you. You're petite and active. And I hate exercise!"

She cried and said she was sorry for yelling at me and being grumpy recently. As the waiter brought the salmon, she asked him for a tissue. I felt guilty because I preferred we'd have a fun and carefree dinner date. Instead, I consoled her for "bad" behaviors of the past.

We discussed wanting kids as early as 2000. There was so much love between us our first two years together that I convinced myself that we should stay together. Plus, I despised the thought of giving up or being alone. When she mistreated me or was in a bad mood, I attributed those behaviors to the stressors of college or work, and, later, to hormones. Maybe therapy and hard work were all we needed to get love back. I could change to fit any mold she thought up. I was confident and adaptable.

Initially, I was not very interested in becoming a parent, but I began to open my mind to the idea. I liked the idea of a family since I loved my own. But I expected Jackie to do most of the child-rearing, not me. I was reasonably unaware of all that was coming towards me. You see, children were Jackie's life, her whole life, above all else. She considered herself a child advocate. Enlisting in the military at 18 to escape her family life and become a nurse, she took on the role of protecting children at a very young age. Being a parent was incredibly important to her. She couldn't wait to have her chance to parent, to show the world how it was done! Raising children, caring for children, and advising other people on how to raise children became her goal, her education, her dedication. One summer evening, we stopped at 7-11 for gas, and a woman was screaming at her kid through the car window, holding a Big Gulp in her hand. The 2-year-old child was inside the car crying. The woman was screaming curse words and pointing her finger at the child. Jackie ran towards them and left me standing at the car. She told the woman to stop yelling. "Can't you see she's just a baby? Knock it off, or I'll call the cops!" The woman opened her door and jumped in her car. Then Jackie turned back towards me, satisfied with her threat. As she got in the car, she said, "Sorry, I do that a lot when kids are threatened!" I was surprised she yelled at the stranger.

She was never impressed with anyone's child-rearing, so she tried to help by babysitting her nieces often. Jackie's niece, Chloe, slept over for 6 or 7 days at a time, which was the most I had been around children. Jackie seemed to know so much more about kids than I did. She took fantastic care of Chloe. I struggled with her. Tested by her kid comments, such as "What do you know about it?" Chloe challenged everything I told her.

"Excuse me?" I turned around in my seat to face her. But Jackie shut me down by putting her hand on my leg and gave me a

51

look to keep me mute.

One morning, as I made breakfast, I offered Chloe a taste of the food. "These are Bellijinkens, our family recipe," I bragged to her. "They're flat pancakes that you put jelly on and roll up."

"Oh gross. Yuck!" Chloe said looking at it and backing up in her chair.

"Well, that's rude. Just try it." I said frowning at her.

"It's okay, Chloe, you don't have to eat it." Jackie quickly dismissed me.

"You can't expect kids to eat what you like just because you like it," she explained in front of Chloe. I didn't know what to say, but I was pissed at both of them.

It was never clear what to do, so I discussed things with Jackie later after Chloe returned to her mom's.

Because I voiced my lack of power, my lack of control and my lack of choices to Jackie, we started going to couples' therapy. Fun, playful activities were never on her agenda, only chores, and tasks! Jackie thought I had plenty of choices and that it was an excuse to prevent myself from being an adult. I said she wasn't fun. And too rigid and controlling a lot of the time. I resented being treated like a child or having my time dictated by Jackie. The therapist said, "Maybe Alison could make plans this weekend instead of you, Jackie." Jackie agreed in the session, but went ahead and kept planning and scheduling everything early without consulting me, even my own family visits to Pennsylvania. Sometimes, setting up activities ahead of time was lovely, but it was the too often. I had absolutely no time of my own. There was no spontaneity, no free days, and no idle time.

After several years of renting the upstairs of a house in

Hadley, we finally invested in our own home in Northampton. I was 30 and Jackie was 32. I was ticking off a to-do-list for my life accomplishments. Looking up the railing of the stairs, I smelled the old wood and fell in love with creaky floors and all the extensive moldings. Initially, I was proud to have a house, and fixing it up was fun. I loved being outside. We both made gardens in the yard. I thought we could slowly improve the grass quality, but Jackie dumped $1,000 for organic lawn people to treat our yard. I could grow grass! They sprayed garlic all over the fence to keep ticks and mosquitos away. It smelled like Mulino's Italian restaurant! They planted grub-killers and seeded the lawn. They said we needed their service every year to get any results! Our house required tons of work in every room, and my stress about money and my "fixing" mindset began to take a toll on my psyche.

Living in a new place took time to acclimate. I used to run down the cellar steps to the boiler and check that it was working properly. It made a horrible sound that rumbled the living room. I worried because the whole house shook when the boiler turned on and off. My family visited from Pennsylvania when we first bought the house. I kept it freezing for January because it made me so nervous. I freaked out when someone in my family blasted the heat. Even though the boiler was inefficient and ancient, Jackie griped, "The old boiler is fine! We can't get you a new one just because you're anxious. You're *always* anxious about things." Getting heat in the house became my extravagant need, not hers.

I loved repairing things, but it was exhausting after years of it. I hated all the cold air flowing through the windows. So I resolved to get four new windows for one room in the house, but Jackie again thought of this purchase as another extravagant desire and not a necessity. We struggled over where to spend our money. I always supported her massages and her electrolysis, but I was getting screamed at for buying home improvements.

Another example was the foundation. I measured the steps and watched as the entire foundation was gradually sinking into the ground. Several contractors confirmed my fears, but we did nothing about it. "It's fine," she said, "we need a new rug in the living room." She blew it off as another anxiety of mine, insisting that I was exaggerating.

One summer day, we bought a tall, aluminum ladder to reach our gutters. Before purchasing the ladder, I had agreed to climb up and clean the gutters, as Jackie had no desire to do it herself. But when we set up the wobbly ladder, I could see it sliding back and forth, left and right, on the gutter, and I told Jackie, "There's no way I'm going up there. It's too damn high and too damn unsafe. Look at the ladder moving!"

Angry and bullying, she yelled, "You *told* me you would go and you *promised* me that you would clean the gutters!"

With fire in my gut and anxiety in my heart, I yelled bravely, "Well, I'm a woman, and it's my prerogative to change my mind!!" All of us are allowed to change our minds at any time.

The Ocean Through a Seashell

Through means to move in one side and
out of the other side of (an opening, channel, or location).

Making a baby was the most adult decision two lesbians endure! The first thing we needed to make a baby was sperm and sperm costs money. "Well, we can just try to get pregnant when we have enough saved to pay for the sperm," I offered sensibly. The hole in our bank accounts was getting larger. "No, we will try EVERY month, no matter what! We can't do this halfway, or it won't work!" Jackie insisted. And so we began the monthly payments and debts associated with trying over and over and over, unsuccessfully, to get pregnant. About $200 each time we tried. I resented yet another decision. Panic rushed through my body as our costs increased. How could I prevent Jackie's dream for children because of money? I couldn't do it. So we ordered monthly from a gay sperm bank because we were committed to having a gay donor. We searched through the profiles. We picked a man we didn't know based on height, weight, eye color, and hair color, unnerving. No photos??? No psychological testing??? The colossal silver metal contraption it arrived in was ridiculous. White smoke came out the top and a tiny, tiny, I mean tiny, plastic tube of sperm was frozen inside. It had to be warmed up and then inseminated into Jackie. A few times, deliveries came too late for ovulation day. One time, I ran down the steps and chased a Fed Ex truck down the street on foot, because they never delivered the sperm on time. Fed Ex finally brought it three days late. The sperm was no longer viable. Thanks for the box. Timing is indeed everything with sperm. Everything!

The other story was the eggs. We wanted to inseminate at home. After many attempts, we realized Jackie needed surgery to get her tubes to open to release the eggs. Then we ultimately realized she wasn't making enough eggs either. She started on Clomid, a drug to help create eggs. Sitting in different doctors' offices was exhausting. One of our first fertility doctors kept telling us to adopt, to which Jackie took offense. She was dedicated to carrying and birthing and nursing her own baby, so adopting wasn't a viable option for her.

After two years and more than fifteen attempts, we were finally pregnant! It felt like we crossed the finish line with both arms high. All the therapy, the moods, the tears, the doctors, the miscarriage, the sperm banks, the donor profiles, the relatives that doubted we should have kids. We did it! We held each other up through the tough times, and we made it.

"Thum-thub, thum-thub, thum-thub" was the heartbeat sound, through the at-home fetal heart monitor, in our bed of blankets and pillows, the smell of bed linens and gel on Jackie's belly. We rented a monitor to check if our baby was still alive. We checked in bed twice a day, or sometimes more. Jackie lifted her shirt, exposing her belly, and I squeezed a glob of gel onto her navel, then I grabbed the telephone like a receiver and unhooked it from the monitor. I'd push it around on her skin, gliding, like pushing a matchbox in no particular direction. You could turn up the volume. It sounded like the ocean through a seashell. Sometimes we didn't hear the thum-thub, then blood drained from our faces.

It was June of 2003 and we had already lost one fetus in week 6 of our pregnancy. We had such a hard time getting pregnant at all that we were devastated by losing the pregnancy. I gravitated to writing poems about our losses. Jackie took it hard, and I tried to comfort her. But I'm not sure Jackie took excellent care of herself, especially in the face of tragedy or struggle. "Everything is harder for me!" She told me through tears in those moments. Jackie had been taking Clomid for over a year, and it only caused crazy mood swings. When we were leaving my parents' house, we were barely out of the driveway when she started bawling, "No one is nice to me there. They are so insensitive to my feelings!" I was so surprised at her emotional state. I thought my whole family was lovely to her! I kept hoping the mood swings were only from the drugs. She never did change back to a sound, steady mood.

One moody evening after having beets for dinner, Jackie panicked at the sight of her pink urine, suspecting a miscarriage. She called me to the bathroom and pointed to the hopper with tears on her cheeks. "Nooooo, it's okay!!!!!" I said enthusiastically. "We had beets for dinner!" Quickly, I flushed her urine away and sat down and peed into a fresh bowl, then stood up. We both leaned cautiously down into the toilet, "See!!! Mine's pink too!!" I said loudly and happily. Jackie laughed and thanked me. It was the exact color pink as hers. It wasn't blood; it was beets in her urine. What a relief!!! But today, we heard 124 beats per minute, thum-thub, thum-thub, thum-thub, still smaller than a peanut yet larger in importance than anything we had ever done in our 30 something years of life.

Creating life was our dream, our common goal. But by the end of July, our second pregnancy, the heartbeat stopped, our hopes snuffed, and the monitor was only the sound of the ocean. I never expected it would be this difficult to attain and hold a pregnancy. Why couldn't pregnancy be natural and easy and stress-free? I was deeply disappointed, but Jackie was truly struck with sadness. For this second miscarriage, we kept the remaining tissues at home. Jackie wanted to have a ritual in the yard to honor the pregnancy, the baby and send good intentions while we bury it. We had a tub of water for cleansing. We dropped the small bloody glob of tissues that came out of Jackie into the water. Slowly, a baby no larger than a golf ball appeared sinking down, down, down into the water, spinning and twirling, with arms and legs, a face, a head, and a tiny body, a face. I had no idea water created a looking glass at the potential baby we might have had. There was a connection formed within me, an unexpected connection from me to my potential baby. It was a hint of a thread to humanity, to emotions, to my future parenthood.

After another miscarriage, and Jackie celebrating another birthday, she felt the pressure and tension of time. She wasn't getting pregnant, and when she did, she had miscarriages. Her stress levels were rising. Both of us were sad and frustrated and exhausted. After our first miscarriage, our long-time friend Anya decided she was going to have a baby too, and got pregnant instantly, and without cost. Of course, we were happy for her and her new baby, yet there was even more pressure building. Anya was our closest friend. She introduced Jackie and I at a music concert, during the time Anya and I attended Springfield College. Anya and Jackie had mutual friends. She was an herbalist and a loving friend to Jackie through our relationship. As the years and the holidays we spent together added up, Anya was like family to both of us.

Getting married was not for both of us. "We can't give the kids your last name unless you marry me," she said. It felt more like a threat than a proposal.

"I don't hold much hope couples stay married in the long term, because of my sister and my brother! They were happy but now both of them are in the middle of messy divorces!" I yelled.

"I will not give my future children your last name unless we are married." She LOVED weddings. She LOVED the image of weddings. I didn't.

Feeling trapped, again I complied. How could I say no? She was struggling with two losses. I thought I had to! I did not weigh my options carefully. It never even occurred to me that I could have resisted or asserted myself by speaking up and legally giving my potential kids my name but not marrying her. But I did marry her, partially because my name was more meaningful than that of Jackie's abusive male relatives, and partly because I wasn't unhappy enough to leave my life. I hated the idea of affecting everyone by asserting myself. I was trying to make the best of what I considered my family. I was committed to my partner of ten years. Dropping the ceiling didn't feel right. I thought things were going to get better or that she might start being nicer and more kind. When I fought against her, it felt like I was the bad guy, especially after the last few years of trying so hard to fulfill the goal of children. If I disagreed with someone I loved, I must be a cruel person. These are the gray areas we rarely acknowledge, the life decisions that count for so much. Here we can blaze new paths for ourselves, by saying, "I'm not ready yet, but let's discuss this," rather than Yes or No. Perhaps I could have offered the option of giving my potential kids my name, but not committing the rest of my life until death do we part. Maybe I liked reacting more than acting on big decisions that felt too large to handle. Maybe handing the responsibility to her felt more comfortable than taking the risk of the lead role. Or maybe at first, I said no to her stipulation, and in the end, acquiesced.

We married at home, in October, on our upstairs porch with Jackie's sister and two nieces and Anya and her baby daughter as witnesses. Our reception included friends of Jackie. There were more than 30 people at our favorite restaurant, The Green Street Café. I was utterly stressed about how we were going to pay for our reception, but we did over many years. We were in debt from college with very little savings. My mind ached with dollar signs.

The highlight was when Anya read a lovely toast as she had been there when Jackie and I first met. I don't remember much of that night. I was terrified and anxious, like watching a car roll away down a hill without any brakes. It didn't seem like my style, none of it. I hated everyone's eyes on me, the judgments. I didn't want a crowd of people watching what felt private in my heart. I suppose I blocked it out. But I do remember that I didn't invite anyone in my family to attend.

After everyone left, we shared a slow dance on the porch where we were married earlier in the day. "I really do love you," she said looking into my eyes. "Me too," I said. "It's just been so hard," she said crying. "Yes, I'm so sorry," I said crying too. We talked about our past worries and our wounds of the ten years we had already spent together. Through miscarriages and trying to get pregnant, we were struggling together, come what may. We spun in circles, apologizing and crying, hoping for happiness in the future. Our tears were made of sadness and suffering, not joy.

Months after the wedding, discussing our many grim events over dinner with Jackie's long-time friends, Seth and Sam, Seth casually offered his sperm to us. "If you guys ever get sick of sperm banks, I could donate to you. I always wanted to create offspring without being a Father," he nonchalantly offered. He had applied to become a sperm donor, but he was rejected due to his short height of five foot, nine inches. We thanked him and then told him we would think about it. We all agreed it could be a great arrangement. I loved that we would know the donor, the more people in the child's life, the better. Seth was excited to have offspring, even if he wasn't planning on playing the father role or raising a child. We discovered that most sperm banks didn't allow gay men to offer sperm. We considered that prejudiced and discriminating. Jackie and I both believed that gay people were as important and as loving as any other person on the planet, and they deserved to create life as much as any other. After thousands of dollars spent on several anonymous donors from cryogenic sperm banks, we preferred and loved the idea of our close friend Seth being a part of our child's genetic makeup, as well as a part of our lives. "I'm excited Seth will be a part of our lives!" I admitted when we talked alone about it. "He will NOT be in our child's life!" Jackie stated loudly. I stared at her as she cried. To be safe, we drafted forms to agree that he would only be a donor and not a father. He and his partner Sam prepared forms that said he had no legal obligation to pay anything over the years. Now, with live sperm, it improved our chances of getting pregnant compared to frozen sperm!

The first time Seth came to our house alone, he had a backpack filled with magazines. He was sweating. Jackie pushed me toward Seth with a sterile jar to put the sperm in. I handed it to him with little small talk. "Thanks," he awkwardly said, "I'll just go into the bathroom and be out in a little bit." "OK," I said back awkwardly, "Thanks!" Jackie hid mostly. I was the courier. After what felt like a lifetime, Seth came out of the bathroom and beelined for the door to leave. Jackie walked him to the door and shoved me toward the jar he left on the bathroom sink. To her, it was sperm getting cold, and she wanted it warm against my body. She whispered, "Go pick it up and put it in your pants." But as Seth drove away, Jackie waited in the bedroom with her pants off, and I had the jar of sperm in my underwear! About 4 or 5 times we did this routine, sometimes at Seth's and sometimes at our house. It was Christmas Eve. Jackie and I were openly laughing and joking as we inseminated. We were hopeful again. The wedding had lifted us. When she peed on the stick two weeks later....we saw two purple lines. We were pregnant again!

Part 3: Parenting

Parenting is when one begets or brings forth offspring;
or brings up and cares for another.

I Saw It with My Heart

The heart is the
central or innermost part of something.

Are you ever really ready to be a parent? We were nervous, first-time parents. I was a nervous person, so yes, I was a nervous parent. Defining my ideas for raising children and standing firm in my role as a mother had not happened yet. I was following Jackie's lead, even after our first baby was born. Jackie always wanted kids more than I did. She seemed to have more confidence than I did, especially since she worked in Pediatrics. "I'm a pediatric specialist," she regularly repeated to me and others. Even to my parents, even to hers. Even to my siblings and her siblings who already had children. As if anyone should ever feel comfortable enough to refer to themselves as an expert on kids. We had been living together for many years, but we didn't marry until the fall of 2004 when same-sex couples could marry legally in Massachusetts. By January 2005, we were pregnant for the third time and again expecting a new life to begin.

Until the baby came, I tried to set myself back into the comfortable rhythm of my life. Work was where I let off steam and spouted off in comical ways. Laughing was my release. I was glad to get out of Jackie's plans and get my freedom at work! On a typical workday, I did "stand-up" and told animated, vivid stories in my cubicle or ranted about funny life events. My seven colleagues stood around me cackling, sometimes crying. I milked the laughter; it fed me. Most of my stories were honest experiences where I needed different perspectives. I enjoyed being open about my view, to make space for my friends to be open and honest with their opinions.

Those seven women at my workplace grew to be my closest friends because of our candidness. Most of the time, I was frank with them about my opinions and my concerns. In a world that traditionally welcomes children to one mom and one dad, things were uncomfortable early on. These women knew me. They knew my doubts about becoming a parent, my insecurities about being a mom. I didn't feel very nurturing. They worried about my parenting skills right away. I spent a lot of time making fun of myself, sometimes referring to my "boy brain." My own gender bias was stereotyping myself into being less nurturing, less thoughtful, less emotional, less worried, more engineer-minded than most women. They were sweet about me being different from them because I was gay, but we stumbled into moments of unexpected awkwardness. Questions popped out quickly. Family-making seemed to strike a vital chord. They seemed to worry about me so much more than any other new moms.

"What if you have a boy? Have you thought about that?" one of them asked. Even I still held the traditional belief that couples and families including a mom and a dad.

"I don't know," I answered innocently.

They pressed on, "Don't you think a boy will need a father figure? I mean, I'm just being honest. Have you thought how your child might feel? Don't you think kids deserve both a father and a mother?"

"No, I don't think so. Many kids don't have a father in their household. I think having two grown-ups is more supportive than only one, but single parents raise healthy kids too." I said, not really knowing the statistics.

"Are you afraid your kid will be made fun of because they have gay moms? Aren't you worried you're putting them at risk for hate crimes right off the bat?" one person asked.

"No, they are growing up in a town where most of the parents were diverse, and many of them were two lesbian moms or two gay dads!" I responded.

Another friend spouted, "Isn't that why God made you gay? You're not really supposed to have kids, are you?"

If these were my friends' comments, I wondered what strangers might be saying. They tried to hold back, but in the end, they started truly asking personal questions that most people don't ask other parents. As if parenting were their territory and my wish for a family was too far over an invisible line. It felt like a shooting range or a test that I hadn't studied for. My mind filled with fears and doubts. Suddenly I represented a much larger group of people than I expected. Who am I to represent the gay parent population? What would my family be like with two Moms, two women raising kids? Is that such a different idea to our conventional society? Why was it assumed that my son needed a father more than my daughter? Aren't most women the ones raising the kids? Why if two women were in love and raising their kids was it different than two sisters raising kids? What is it about humans that put such expectations on parenting? Am I only a good mom if I'm married to a man? Am I only contributing to society if I love a man? Why?

Love makes a family. Conventional role-playing isn't essential in the life of a child. Confidence in parenting is MOST important for me. Parents supporting other parents are crucial. People helping other people are important for families. Forming loving relationships is the best thing we can do for our kids. The connection between humans doesn't have anything to do with femininity or masculinity, doesn't have anything to do with gender or image, nothing at all. Gender and sexuality can be kept separate from the depth and breadth of relationships.

As a kid, my grandparents were beautiful together because of the connection they had to each other. I wasn't *only* watching a man and a woman in love. It was two friends connecting. Love wasn't found in their clothes or their image or their genitals. Love was the energy lifting them, dancing them, engulfing them in joy and sharing. It was invisible, but I saw it with my heart. I know little boys can identify and relate to women just as well as men and vice versa. I did. Humans get mixed up about how love works. Love isn't made through friction and skin. Love isn't reserved for only a man and a woman. Love is for all of us to enjoy. That's where family begins, in love. Connection grows on an intimate level, being authentic.

At the baby shower, I joked more about who would breastfeed. But my joking left me open to critical concerns such as,

"Are you going to breastfeed or Jackie?" they asked point blank. Then soon they were sorry they asked.

"No, I don't want to be that sort of mom."

Then they inquired more, "What kind of mom will you be?"

"I'm not the kind that breastfeeds!" I said.

Most of them didn't advocate for breastfeeding. But Anya and Jackie knew that both women could successfully breastfeed by merely taking some hormones and suckling the baby on the breast. Ultimately, a woman's hormones kick-in and lactation begins. The questions quickly turned into a sort of joke about what it might be like to have two moms breastfeeding and how funny that would be, passing the baby breast to breast between us. It felt more like they were making fun of me, rather than supporting me. The traditional roles of mom and dad also became a discussion.

"Is the father going to be involved with your kids? Will he meet them?" someone asked.

"There is no father," I educated them. "We refer to him as a donor because he won't be raising the child at all. He'll be like an uncle or a friend to the child." I informed them. Awkward, they felt scolded; like I was telling them a new rule in an arena they felt dominant. But I was trying to educate them not to refer to the donor as a father.

Stories about their brothers or husbands not helping with raising the kids came up. "You're going to be the one that spoils them!" they said. Discussion about what type of mom I might be came up....I didn't think about it yet. How could I know? How would a child look up to a lesbian mom? Would they think I was a weird mom? What would my kids think of me? I was scared! My parents and relatives considered me strange or odd. Could I be my true self as well as a loving mother? I was trying to sound self-assured to my friends, but I was scared and clueless and filled with doubts.

Not all of my friends were lobbing critical questions at me. Most of them whole-heartedly supported me. Only three of the seven were moms already, two never had kids, and two had their babies after I did. One said, "Alison will be a great mom. Lots of love and a great sense of humor! None of us know what we're getting into when we are first time parents!" Those awkward discussions did help me wake up to some of my upcoming issues. But mostly, I relished talking with them and being real, not holding back or hiding. I appreciated that we were all honest with each other, regardless of the varying emotions. I was ill-prepared and utterly clueless about how to navigate my future as a lesbian mom.

One Thursday, when Jackie was eight months pregnant, I arrived around 9 am to discover that my colleagues, McGee and Wang were already in the office waiting for me. We launched into discussions. As we debated over which type of statistics to use to analyze the data, a nervous Greta knocked on the door and said, "I'm so sorry to interrupt, but Jackie called and told me to send you home because she is having the baby NOW."

McGee looked at me with big eyes and said, "GO GO GO!!" I apologized as I ran through the cubicles grabbed my bag and ran to the parking garage. Jackie had an appointment with the midwives that morning, but we had assumed it would be fine. The baby had been upside down in the uterus, so Jackie had taken homeopathic medicine to get her to flip head down. Now the baby was down. Our midwife felt her cervix already dilated at seven centimeters. Passing cars at 80 mph, I dialed Jackie. She was incredibly calm. She told me not to rush home; it could still be weeks until the baby came out. "Don't worry," she said, as she stirred the chicken soup she was making. She had already prepared a bag to take to the birthing center as I drove south like a bolt of lightning.

Over the phone, the midwives were telling us her water could break at any moment and to be prepared to head to the birthing center within the next 24 hours. Contractions were strange and sudden and scary. My fears and doubts began to creep in on me. I didn't have much trust in whether the baby would be healthy, whether Jackie's health would be compromised, whether I'd lose both the baby and Jackie. I was so fearful of all the unknown events that could happen during childbirth that I couldn't stop a constant stream of what-ifs from plaguing me. "What if you go into labor in the car?" I asked. "What if I can't find you in the birthing center?" I asked Jackie.

Because I was nervous and we weren't sure if she was having actual contractions, we drove to the hospital, only a few miles from our house. Anya, Jackie's best friend was invited for the birth also. She was an herbalist and was like family to us. She began dosing out Rescue Remedy to calm our nerves. We opened our mouths like birds, and she grinned and squirted it in.

At 4:30 pm, Jackie's contractions were still weak and scattered, not consistent. Nina, our birthing midwife, told us "I've done this a million times. It's all normal. The baby just isn't ready to come out yet." She radiated confidence and experience.

But just before she was going to send us back home, Nina decided to assess Jackie's cervix and discovered that it was nine centimeters dilated. She wasn't comfortable sending us home with an opening that wide, so now we had to stay at the hospital after all.

Jackie told them she wanted everything to happen naturally. So we waited overnight into the next day to try to see if her water would break on its own. I didn't sleep at all that night, wondering, *Why did we wait? What's going to change between tonight and tomorrow?* I was so impatient!

While we waited, I asked Jackie if we could tell Seth that she was in labor. We had already been waiting for hours, so I thought it would be easy enough to make a phone call. But she refused, shaking her head 'no.' I sighed and slouched in my chair. *Why is it such a big deal to call him?* I had a feeling Seth would want to know. I liked that he was excited about the baby coming.

The doctor showed up by morning and discussed options with us. At 10 am they broke the water sac and began medicine to bring on contractions. Now the midwife Nina was off duty and on came Stacey! We loved her immediately also. Stacey's eyes stayed locked on us; she touched our hands from time to time. Her demeanor was calm and grounded. She listened tentatively to our concerns and questions. Plus the nurse Angie was cheesy and outspoken, saying things like, "All of us here love you, and we will be here supporting you and rubbing your body throughout this miracle of birth!"

Another miracle happened that day; I posed a question to Jackie that proved important. I cleared my throat and took a deep breath, leaning on Jackie's shoulder as she sat up in the birthing bed. Before the contractions got worse, I needed to tell her something. "I don't want to be called Lama or Rama or some other odd name that doesn't show the world that I'm their mother too." I winced as I said it and waited for her reaction. Without truly planning this out, I took the opportunity because she was more likely to say 'yes.' The likelihood of her listening to me was better in a public place. At the last possible second, I finally realized I wanted to be Mom, just like Jackie was, and equally important. I wasn't a father, and I wasn't just another relative. I needed to be Mom also. "I want my kid to call me 'Ma'" I said. "It's similar to my name 'Al' and I call my Mom, 'Ma' all the time. So what do you think of 'Ma' for me?" "Well," she slowly gazed behind me. I think she stalled to scan the room for listeners. I stared directly into her eyes, somewhat scared for her reaction. "OK," she said. Then she twinkled and laughed a little. "I can't believe you're telling me this now! You waited until the last possible second!" "Yeah, I know, but it dawned on me during all these office visits and things that none of the nurses knew what to call me. I realized the significance of a label that is as universally understood and important as 'Mom.' It's important that I'm a mom too, especially to my child!" With that decision settled, her contractions began, the baby decided to meet us finally.

The baby's heart rate never wavered at 140 bpm, keeping us very comfortable the entire birth. By 2 pm we added more and more Pitocin but otherwise a natural childbirth. Watching the contractions come over Jackie was painful to witness. She was not in charge. She surrendered to the labor pains, not unlike an orgasm. The squeezing took hold of her and moved her. She arched and moaned. Angie said, "Don't push yet! Hold on Jackie…a little bit longer!" Jackie would buckle and yell and say, "Don't touch me." Finally, by 5:30 pm she began actively pushing the baby out. Eventually, and quickly the contractions were close and strong enough to push this baby out. The room became about the contractions. All of us worked as a team. A wave of energy began and peaked as she pushed. Squatting, kneeling, or laying down, Jackie tried positions to drop the baby down. Our nurse, Angie, was still talkative, loud, barking out strange thoughts to Jackie like, "Hold on to yourself! Ride the wave! It may feel like a painful wave, but you are not alone! We are *with* you!" She was also very attentive to Jackie and focused on ice and rags to cool her down. Jackie just kept saying, "Oh God. Oh God," and thought she might throw up a few times. She never did though. Each push lasted 10 or 12 seconds, Anya holding one leg and I holding the other.

The baby's head finally began to crown. The bulge of the baby showed and pushed and ripped at Jackie's skin. The crowning head motivated me, Anya, Angie, and Stacey to yell, "Yes. Yes. Yes. That's it!! That's it!!" Jackie knew what it felt like when she pushed hard enough to get it out. The tension was rising with the succession of contractions. It was 7:30 pm when I looked at the clock and wondered when we would finally have a baby in the room with us, in the space with us, in the flesh with us.

We didn't know it was a girl, but we both guessed it was. We had a feeling. Angie began repeating, "One more push. Just one more! That baby's head is about to turn and come out!!" As Jackie and the baby turned purple from all the pressure, the moment built and grew and swelled, and the baby was about to crown out. The baby's little black head of hair was surfacing more and more. Angie was yelling now, "Push for your baby, Jackie. Push. Push for all of womankind!" I couldn't laugh, but I also couldn't believe some of the things Angie was saying. Then it seemed quiet. I looked up, and no one was there but Anya and I each grabbed a leg . . . Where did everybody go?

Double doors flew open, as they were quickly running back in with tables and equipment and raincoats on, sterilized and ready for tiny the baby's arrival. As the baby bulged more and more, Angie squirted AstroGel on its head to make for a more slippery exit. "AstroGel? That's a funny name!" I said, and all the nurses and the midwife laughed out loud.

Then: ears to ankles, zoom! The baby flopped right out, wet and tired, onto the paper-covered delivery table. No one caught her. Our baby dove into this world! Stacey scooped her up onto Jackie's chest and began suctioning her mouth and ears and nose. As women swarmed the baby and Jackie, I was pushed backward and away from the bed, stunned. *There it is! We had a child! There's a baby here!* Then I stepped forward to push through the crowd. Jackie reached for me, and as I got closer to both of them, I saw a scissor handle sticking out to cut the umbilical cord, so I squeezed it.

"Is it a girl or a boy?" Jackie asked.

Angie finally reached over and spread our child's legs. "It's a girl," she said.

I knew it! I thought. "Is it healthy?" I asked Jackie. I stared at the baby; her eyes were going in different directions, her skin was pale pink, and she was covered in white stuff. Her duck-like lips were flappy, her head funny shaped.

Jackie's mouth curled up, and she said, "Yes she's normal. She's healthy. It's all okay!"

I hugged both of them, not sure how to act toward this new, googly-eyed creature.

Maria was born on August 19, 2005, at 7:47 pm She was one month early and tiny—only six pounds, three ounces—but healthy.

During the waiting time and after the birth, I told Jackie a few times to call and tell Seth. "No," she'd say, "I don't have to yet." But I still wanted to call and share the good news every day after. Finally, several days later, she called him to tell him she had a baby girl. Two weeks later we went down to visit Sam and Seth, and he pulled me aside. "You could have at least called to tell me she was born. It was just a phone call."

He didn't listen for my response; he just assumed I withheld the information, not Jackie. Did he think it was *my* decision not to call him? Was he too intimidated by Jackie to confront her? Did he assume I should have been the person who called since Jackie was giving birth? He was so disappointed in me, yet I'm the one who had tried to get her to call him. I was the one who wanted to tell him. How could I blame Jackie, when I could have called him? I was stuck with Jackie insisting that I not call and my gut feeling that we should have told him Maria was born.

911

911 are the numbers to call
for help in an emergency.

The baby slept on Jackie for day naps and at night. Jackie decided to
co-sleep. We had a crib, but Maria never slept in it. So making love or
being close was nonexistent. Maria and Jackie were close and stayed
that way. I was the gopher. I followed Jackie's instructions on
everything. Slowly, I grew more comfortable holding her. She was
tiny and easy to put in the baby wrap. We had a huge ball I bounced
her on for her to sleep or relax. Intimate moments staring at her and
feeling her warmth filled me with love. Fuzzy-headed and soft skin,
she fit in my palms perfectly, as I held her against my chest and
rocked. There was such awe in being seen holding Maria and receiving
all that love and advice from strangers was astounding. "Enjoy her!"
they all said, "Love her to pieces, even after she learns to talk back!"
Some people hugged both of us. Maybe that was what it was like to be
pregnant and have people touch your belly. Many people said, "Is she
your first? OOOHHHH how precious!!! Congratulations Mom!" I
loved the attention and the giving and receiving of love energy. I wore

a permanent glow.

As a newborn, Maria was jaundice and needed a billy blanket to lower her bilirubin levels. The hospital gave us a billy blanket with lights in it to reduce her bilirubin levels at home, but eventually, her levels kept climbing, so we had to put her into an incubator type bed with blue lights. When we got to the hospital, Jackie knew what would happen. She was familiar and comfortable in the clinical setting, but I was scared and wanted to leave. As I stood next to the tiny bed, I broke open, trying to hide my tears from everyone. Uncomfortable with revealing my tears, I tried desperately to hold myself together. Fear crept into my throat and won the fight. Soon I couldn't stop crying. Jackie looked at me blankly. "It's not a big deal," she whispered. The nurses consoled me, then brought me a chair and a box of tissues and pushed me closer to Maria's bed. Once I was crying, there was no stopping it. I sat like a child in a big lounge chair and watched as my baby girl slept in a little blue light bed. She looked so innocent and small that I couldn't catch my breath between sobs, a pile of tissues beside me on the chair. The feelings inside my body made me ache. It was a mix of surrender and fear from not being able to help my new baby. It was the first time I let myself truly realize my vulnerability through her. I couldn't heal her. I couldn't help her or even hide my feelings. Only a few months after her arrival, and already, I couldn't protect her. Feeling that helpless made me fall to pieces. We brought her home after one overnight in the blue light bed. She was fine after that.

I was incredibly proud of my baby. There's a piece of me that got stupid over her. Seeing other parents act silly made me laugh, but now it was me playing the part of the fool! She was cute and animated, and I loved showing her off. One time, when she was about six months, I stopped on the sidewalk to show our closest friend Cheryl and another friend how cute Maria was. The three of us bent over and peered under the hood of the stroller at Maria. I prompted her by flirting with her and saying, "Smile! Who's a cutie-girl!?! Come on, Maria, smile!"

At that, my friend Cheryl, remarked sarcastically to her friend, "Jump, monkey, jump!" Apparently, she felt I was making my baby perform for them. *What did she say? Did she say something mean to me?*

I searched Cheryl's face to see a sign of warmth or jest, but no, nothing. *How can she not see how much I love my child?* She didn't see me. She wasn't looking at me. She looked at her friend and rolled her eyes, her mouth smirked. Hurt, I lost all motivation to spend time with Cheryl ever again.

"Working" was almost impossible while caretaking. Telecommuting was my primary goal. Parenting should have been my primary goal, loving my child. I had already worked from home once a week, and when Maria came, I took a second day to raise my child. My life depended on being with my kid and keeping my job. I worked for the state, and the benefits were outstanding! The pay was excellent, and I loved my job, my co-workers, and the flexible hours. Feeding Maria pumped breast milk with a bottle was tough too. She wanted Jackie, not me. I'd fumble with the refrigerated bags, heat up the bottles, wash the bottles after feedings. I was in charge of cleaning the breast pump and putting the breast milk away and labeling the bags. I hadn't realized all the details involved in child-rearing.

Time management got more and more challenging as she

grew and needed more love and attention than a newborn. The phone rang, and they needed me to run statistics or suddenly have a meeting at the same time Maria needed to go down for a nap. It was stressful. Maria and I played in between my work. I was always on the laptop. She pulled out her Fisher Price laptop and worked next to me. "Ma, I want your pink phone," she took my pink flip phone and pretended to talk to Mama on it. Naturally, she didn't understand when I needed to get my work done. "Please Ma, Please Ma, Pleeeeeeeease Ma!! Hold me!!" she said clinging to my calves as I typed at the kitchen island. Dinner was on, the phone ringing, emails soaring at my head. Often, Maria needed me to comfort her, but I was stressed and closed up, not able to convey affection. Sometimes I flipped out because I couldn't get to my work and care for her at the same time. Forgiving me for those moments of anger took years.

I was new at all of this! Being responsible and keeping my daughter alive kept me so very stressed as a first-time mom. I assumed she would die if I didn't keep an eye on her always, especially, when I was left alone with her. My childhood involved little to no younger children. I never did babysit as a teenager. Jackie was as scared as I was when I was alone with Maria. Luckily, we taught her sign language early to help us know what she needed. I thought she was a GENIUS!

"Aren't they all?" one of my elder volunteers said winking, "Aren't they all?!"

With Maria, I tried to think ahead, to avoid errors, always knowing Jackie's judgments were lurking when she got home. Jackie set up the standards, the rules, the expectations. Run protectively alongside Maria's plastic car to avoid injuries. Remember to soak her cloth diapers immediately to get them clean. Don't put any plastic cups in the dishwasher. Don't forget to wash out and soak the breast pump hoses and bottle lids in the warm soapy water immediately upon arrival. The backlash was ugly. Jackie's reactions were loud. "How many times do I have to tell you?!?! Soak the pump!"

As I prepared to go somewhere, I often got the dog in the back of the SUV first, then situate my baby into her car seat. But then I walked back to the house to fetch another forgotten item before leaving the house on an errand. I went back for the leash, the ball, the favorite doll, the binkie, the diaper bag, the blankie, the water bottle— whatever it was, I forgot it first, then I remembered it and went back. My self-loathing grew with each forgotten item. Jackie never liked what I did or how I did it because it was different than what she would choose to do. It seemed like we could use a few things to alleviate our stress a bit, but I was alone in that thought as well. Disposable diapers? Easy cleaning? Simple meals? Put plastic in the dishwasher? Taking the baby spoon from my hand, Jackie said, "Let me do it. This is how you do it," and then showed me how to feed the baby "correctly."

"We each do it differently," I said.

But she considered any different approach downright wrong.

"No, she'll choke if you do it your way," she insisted.

Maria got sick several times during the first two years of her life, and I don't know why. Vomiting with fever, she got weak and looked at me with her big brown eyes and said, "Ma, can you hold me?" Then I ached as she passed out in my arms from the illness and exhaustion. My heart hurt to be close to such a fragile baby girl. I didn't want to be too close to such a love, for fear of breaking, but I didn't want to be separate either. This was new to me, the trouble with love. Part of me tried to resist this connection. I took on her feelings into my own body. When she was feverish, so was I. When she had stomach aches, so did I. When she had any pain, so did I. As I walked exhausted up the stairs to the bedroom with some books to read for Maria one night, Jackie said, "Alison, Alison!!!!!" With such fear and screech in her voice that I thought Maria's head must have exploded. "Whaaaat?!?! Whaaaat!?! I yelled back, half joking, to Jackie in the same frantic screech as I ran up the stairs two at a time. Maria had just thrown up, but Jackie's fear and anxiety were truly freaking me out. "She's OK," I told Jackie when I went in the room. She was already stripping the bed, standing on the mattress, sheets and covers flying. I could see then, that Jackie was emotionally flipping out. After months of nonstop parenting with rarely any breaks besides naptime, we were both emotionally unraveling.

"Wake up, Ma!" said Maria around 18 months. She kissed my eyes and cheeks to wake me up in the morning. "I love you!" she said all morning and all day long. She leaned over me, head-heavy and puckered up her tiny lips for a kiss. She danced with me daily, shifting her weight left to right, wiggling her hips. It took me time to relax into being responsible for her little life. Dancing to music was my best strategy to relieve my stress during my 12 hour days alone with her. One day, I heard Maria saying "Tweet, tweet, Ma! Tweet, tweet!" from the living room. A sparrow flew in through the window. I pulled Maria onto my hip and tried shooing it away with my hand. It landed on my kitchen counters and pooped everywhere. She kept pointing and saying "tweet Ma, tweet!" I opened the front door, and it finally flew away. "Bye, bye birdy!" Maria waved from my arms.

I rarely took my eyes off Maria at first. At night, I stood next to her bed when she finally drifted off to sleep. Watching her small body rise and fall with each breath, her soft cheeks, her long, long eyelashes, the wrinkles in her chubby arms, she was so new and innocent. I stared at her and daydreamed about how she was created, who she would be, what she would do in her lifetime?

Often we videotaped Maria because she liked performing for us. She never wanted to be the center of the attention in any room around other folks, but she wanted both her Moms' attention constantly. "Ma! Look!! Ma!!! See me?!?! Watch this!!!" Leaping and twirling, then we clapped. She showed off for us, always dancing and performing.

During that time, we were in Maine on a much-needed summer vacation, when Maria spiked a fever several times. We crawled from nap to nap to get a break from the caretaking. Jackie kept taking off all Maria's clothes and taking her outside to help the fever come down. I begged her to see a doctor, but she insisted they couldn't do anything for teething. But after about four days of low-grade fever, we finally took her to the ER at York. She was diagnosed with strep throat. Jackie didn't agree with antibiotics or vaccinations and resisted any such medicine at first, but she eventually conceded to the doctor's recommended dose of antibiotics and Maria's fever disintegrated.

Jackie's rigid opinions began worrying me after that vacation of suffering. Why did we have to sacrifice our child? We weren't the type of health care professionals ever to overuse antibiotics or vaccines. That's why I couldn't understand Jackie's stubbornness on this issue. "Why can't we just take her to the doctor?" I asked her angrily. "Because her body is strong, she can fight off a little fever! They can't do anything for her that I can't do for her!" she said, always verbally hitting me with, "I wish you would trust me!"

Stubbornness can be viewed in a more positive light when referred to as willful. My daughter was adaptable and willful. Maria fearlessly climbed up the tree house I built for her, the red rungs on the ladder, the green wood for the floor. Hands deep in my pockets, I would be focused and strained, brows furrowed, barking out, "Be careful" or "Slow down" or "Not too high" I'd say over and over. She learned young to say, "Ma, stop worrying!" Maria spun CDs on my stereo. I let her put the CD's in herself, and she loved the independence. I also let her pick out my clothes for me. Digging around in my drawer and holding them up. She picked my red corduroys often. She loved shopping since she was little enough to reach the clothes rack. Our child learned early to navigate the extreme parenting styles of Jackie and me. I gave her tons and tons of freedom by letting her lead all the activities and make decisions. But Jackie conducted all the choices for Maria. Mama set up precisely the craft or the paints where she wanted and how she wanted. Mama picked out the clothes she wore. Mama decided the day's activities.

There's something to be said about the learning curve for parenting. I was clueless and scared when Maria and I were alone. At about twelve months, Maria was climbing a ladder one late summer day, when she slipped, bumping her lips against her teeth. She screamed and started crying. I grabbed her up with both arms and peeked into her mouth. It suddenly filled with blood. I tucked her under one arm and frantically ran for a sponge. My heart was pounding. *What if she dies? What if she can't breathe? What if the bleeding doesn't stop?*

It took all of about ten seconds for the bleeding on her lip to subside, but I had already dialed 911. The ambulance showed up within seven minutes, and the EMTs were so kind to me. I casually walked Maria out front to the sidewalk to three lovely young men rushing to what they thought was an emergency. "I'm sorry, you guys—I just freaked out. There was blood."

They just smiled and looked in Maria's mouth and said, "It's OK. She's fine." As they left, one young Dad looked over his shoulder as he walked to the red ambulance, "I get it. I have twin boys. I know how it is. Blood is normal at my house." He laughed.

It was embarrassing, but a good story. My friend Gloria still chuckles and refers to me as "911". After that incident, I realized with deep sympathy my own parent's reaction when I fell on the stick. Kids are fragile and resilient, exciting and terrifying. However, Jackie didn't show sympathy for the incident. When I revealed my anxiety and admitted things like, "I'm not sure what to do when I get scared." Or "Do you think I could get better at parenting?" Jackie responded without compassion, "I think maybe you should take medication for your anxiety." or "Why don't you do something about it? Help yourself!"

Why not support me by merely touching my hand or shoulder, then say, "I would have been scared too." Empathy can lower anxiety. Yet after I told her the whole funny 911 story, she looked at me blankly and said nothing. Similar to my family, there was no discussion of feelings. Maybe she felt more insecure about my abilities because I called 911. Perhaps she never trusted me at all. Either way, the emergency wasn't Maria, it wasn't my child who needed reviving, it was my marriage.

Reduction

Reduction is the action or fact of
making a specified thing smaller or
less in amount, degree, or size.

When Maria turned two, Jackie said, "She needs a sibling."

I disagreed. "Maria doesn't need a brother or sister. She's very particular and likes her two moms to herself," I insisted.

"No!" she yelled. "I don't want her to grow up alone!"

We argued about it for days. I raged on at first, making good points about needing more time, not enough money, not enough support, points that weren't heard at all. Then I talked to my mom about it. "You have to do what she wants," my mom said. "If you can't get her to listen to you, then you have to make peace. You can't keep arguing and fighting," she advised.

Ultimately, we attempted to get pregnant at all costs. After two more miscarriages and over a year and a half of trying to get pregnant our doctor told us we needed a new donor. Jackie told me to call and tell Seth. He was Jackie's friend first. I didn't know him that well. *Talk to a man about the fluid that comes out of his penis? Ok.* My hands were shaking. I kept looking at the phone in disbelief. *What could I say? How could I deliver this news without hurting his feelings?* Sperm was a delicate subject to discuss. I hate hurting people's feelings! I was resentful beyond belief at Jackie. But again, I called Seth rather than exercising my willpower against her. I dialed the phone alone. Seth answered. Abruptly, "I'm sorry to have to tell you this, but our doctor thinks we need a different donor. You have less sperm than you did four years ago and they aren't swimming as well." I exhaled my gum. It was the hardest conversation to have— telling a man he had very little sperm and not enough fast-moving sperm. Silence. I repeated myself. Uttering these words was something I never thought I would say to a man, twice. *Bad sperm. Baaaaad sperm.* I hung up feeling like he didn't understand me.

The phone rang after five minutes. "Are you having a problem with me?" Seth asked. *Nope, just your sperm.* "Because it would help me if you were honest with me." I didn't know how to be more honest than telling him the truth.

"I'm sorry you felt like I wasn't honest," I said. "The doctor told us to get a new donor with a higher sperm count as well as better motility to increase our chances. We're just trying to increase our chances of getting pregnant. It has nothing to do with you! We prefer you! We wanted you to be the donor of BOTH our kids!" I reassured him. People hear their own truth sometimes.

After trying for a year or so for additional siblings, Jackie moved on to in vitro fertilization. Unknown donors and back to searching through cryogenic profiles for the perfect man. They did a procedure to harvest Jackie's eggs and then combine it in a tube with unknown donor sperm. The eggs were fertilized. They implanted 3 or 4 fertilized eggs in Jackie's uterus. She was crying and groggy wearing a Johnnie when they harvested her eggs. After two attempts over four months, we were pregnant with three baby boys. *Triplets!* We could hear the heartbeats, three of them.

Triplets were a windfall. We had a big family coming! Part of me, after almost two years of trying, had grown more resigned to letting the universe decide about the number of siblings for Maria. When the results showed three....I thought we were extremely LUCKY! A whole group of boys! They told us when we inseminated as a side note, we could have a reduction or reduce the number of fetuses, but I thought they meant early, like right when they first implanted to the uterus. The word *reduction* had meant nothing then, nothing. But now it meant we had the option to eliminate fetuses in a doctor's office with a syringe, not unlike an abortion. The worst was being told we had to wait until they grew for at least twelve more weeks! What a nightmare? We were getting more and more attached to three babies only to destroy some of them physically? I ached with every detail of it. What would Jackie decide? I thought it would be impossible to carry these babies for three more months without growing attached and then reduce them. But I was wrong.

When the doctor casually sat us in front of a computer showing a PowerPoint presentation with the chances of survival of triplets, I was fuming and sick and scared. "The survival rates are 30% higher when you reduce from triplets to twins." He advised. Most people want to increase their chances of keeping the children as well as reduce the strain on your own body by reducing or killing one fetus of the three.

"I'd like to reduce down to one baby," Jackie said. I was shocked. I had assumed we were having twins. I prayed she would come to her senses. I had no words. We had the chance to have three sons, and she was stealing away a baby, or two.

We rode in the car in silence at first, thinking, stunned. Then, as we approached home, I said, "Okay, it is, after all, your body, not mine, so you have to be the one to decide. But please, please consider twins, at least think about it," I said. She just cried and looked out the window.

I dwelled on it though, journaling my hopes and dreams for love, writing about a different reality. I slowly changed my thinking on everything. As Jackie created and built different beliefs, I adapt to each one. I agreed with her because I thought I was being a good partner, a supportive wife. I thought if I could keep agreeing with her, it would maintain peace and love in our relationship. At first, I figured after having kids; things would get easier, and then I thought, if I helped her more often, it would get easier. Later, I thought things would be easier if she had more kids. Or maybe if I agreed with her more and backed up her decisions, things would get easier. I'll support the reduction because it's safer for Jackie's health. I was sacrificing my own choices and feelings, stuffing my true beliefs down again. Poof! I was falling away, making excuses on the way down, disappearing, putting our relationship before myself. But as for Jackie's emotions, I still tried to anticipate them, and I called that love.

She, as usual, was confident that she didn't want too many siblings to take away from Maria. "No, Maria wouldn't like two or three siblings! Maria won't want *that* many boys taking away her time from us!" she insisted. Her confidence overshadowed my doubts. She won.

Digesting all this was difficult enough, as life handed us circumstances that reached too far into the future. Jackie rebelled and pushed back with each decision. Threading a needle for her ideal situation, it seemed impossible to make her happy. I originally wanted to leave well enough alone. Don't try to get pregnant again! Maria was still growing and changing. If siblings were meant to be in our family, Jackie's wish would come true. When three babies were suddenly growing, it was meant to be. I believed in life happening without our steering and interfering. Leave it alone. It's not in my control, so I adapted to the changing situations. Live and let live. Who am I to determine exactly how things were meant to play out?!? It seemed much too controlling to implant three fertilized eggs and then kill off exactly the ones we chose. I didn't agree with all this science determining our destiny. Jackie's decisions were contradictory to our natural, organic lifestyle. All her credibility was deteriorating. She had always told me she wouldn't do infertility drugs, but now she was. Why was she making these decisions? Was she afraid? When will she begin to accept life on life's terms?

After years of arguing about not wanting a sibling, now so many possibilities blessed us! I was so disappointed that she could actually kill off two fetuses, our fetuses, the ones we asked for and paid for and prayed for! I was angry to the core, and the anger expanded in my body. I could have done more to try and convince Jackie, but part of me wanted the excuse to hate her. I kept wondering, why and how she could abort or reduce? Perhaps she was scared for her life. She had shown me she was selfish in the past, but this was incredibly selfish. I couldn't imagine pushing so hard to have siblings and then reducing not one baby, but two. Wow. I was in a daze. "How do you choose which one to abort?" I asked the doctor tearing up.

"We will check that they are all healthy prior to the procedure," he answered. What a horrible thing to have to choose! Every one of the three of them was healthy. I was terrified of losing all three by reducing to one. We should leave it to God, to the universe, to something bigger than us, not to Jackie. Jackie was clear on her decision, although it made her cry a lot. Jackie's decision was one more example of her playing the martyr. I hated her choosing to suffer, and she knew it.

The lights were fluorescent and unforgiving as we sat in a room full of strangers waiting to have medical procedures, such as a reduction. Most of the women there were pregnant and expecting, sitting with their husbands or boyfriends. We didn't see any other same-sex couples. Fidgeting in my chair, I tried to take care of Jackie and her feelings. "Are you okay?" I asked for the tenth time.

"I'm fine," she whispered looking down at the tissue in her hand. She had been crying softly for days. I could feel my heart pounding in my ears, tightness in my belly. How could we go through with this? I was nauseous! Part of me was humbled that Jackie had the courage to go through with this procedure. Scared and worried, it felt like hours and hours when they finally called us in to wait in another room. Staring at walls with teen pregnancy posters, we were feeling ridiculous, sitting on tables with rolled out white paper. Why do we wait so much longer when we are anxious?

Finally, we went into a room with a large overhead projector on the wall. The doctor and two nurses were covered in clinical white.

We had never seen or met any of these medical staff before today. The doctor specialized in reductions. "I know this is a hard thing to do. Don't think the reason you are here is lost on me. We'll try to be as fast, gentle, and informative as we can. But I suggest not looking at the projection up on the wall. It's going to show me a picture of the three babies so I can reduce the two closest to the outside of the uterus. The one in the middle will be your baby to grow to full term. Do you have any questions?"

Jackie asked in a high-pitched teary voice, "Is there any risk to our baby by reducing the other two?"

"No." he answered. "I do this all the time, and no harm will come to the other baby. The procedure is simple and only takes 10 minutes. Are you ready?" We both nodded. I grabbed Jackie's hand and closed my eyes tight. Surrendering to fate, I buried my head down into her ribs. She was lying down on the table with an ultrasound machine on her stomach. I couldn't resist peeking. I blinked my eyes at the projection on the wall, and I saw a small fetus reacting to the needle inserted into its center. It looked like pain. The needle made the fetus fold tight. His tiny feet went up. His tiny head down. It was a quick flash, but I was even more nauseous after seeing what we had chosen to do. I closed my eyes tighter, pinching away the sight, pinching away my guilt. This was not my choice. We had gone through so many losses, yet now, here we were, doing the unthinkable. I've always been pro-choice, not pro-life, but seeing the reduction was too clinical and too barbaric for me. I can often see both sides of most arguments, but now I have more compassion for how honestly hard these decisions are for human beings. My mind flooded with questions and doubts. What if these triplets were a product of rape? Would we feel better about eliminating them? What if they were unhealthy? What if Jackie was healthy enough to bring two or three babies to full term? What if we lose the one baby after getting rid of the other two? Would Maria be "better off" with twin brothers? How will our relationship weather this decision over time? Where do the souls of these fetuses go? Will our baby feel the absence of his brothers? Aren't these decisions too big for us? What's the right choice? What if I was the one pregnant and had to decide? Should I have fought harder for the twins?

We went home and just cried. I shut down, and part of me died. I grew closed and hollow, numb. We each healed separately. To feel better, I played guitar, while Jackie straightened up the house. Jackie knew I wasn't happy with her choice to reduce, although most of her guilt was self-inflicted. They told us whatever physiological parts of our two lost boys would simply disappear and absorb back into Jackie's body without much bleeding. We absorbed them. Our couple's therapist told us to focus on our living baby and let the other two go. It was time to move on now. One night, we lit a candle to honor our lost boys and their existence with a small flame as a form of acknowledging them and letting them go.

A Strange and Ominous Energy

Ominous is giving the impression
that something bad or unpleasant
is going to happen; threatening.

Sharing the fact that Jackie was pregnant with Maria helped to make it more real for us. Maria's eyes looked up at us in anticipation of good news. "You're going to have a little brother!" we both told her together at the dinner table through tears and smiles. Maria bent sideways in her chair and looked sick, "I….I….I don't know what's happening to me…." Is all she could say. "Its OK honey, we don't have to talk about it now. You can talk about something else now," Jackie told her. Maria got up and went to play with her toys in a silent daze. I looked worried at Jackie across the table as she tried to hide her tears.

Getting his bedroom ready was another practical part of nesting. It helped our hope overcome the sadness. Sadness helps move me to action, to get better. When I feel that low, that depressed, I tend to fight against the misery of the feeling. I get motivated to climb out of the hole, to do something, anything. Sometimes the extreme contrast of misery with joy makes it easier to move a couple notches closer to joy, even if you never actually reach joy at all.

We wanted to reach Noah, our son. Birthing him safely was still our mutual goal. Both of us were still worried there would be another shoe to drop, something unforeseen. After several more months, we met with Jenna, one of the midwives. We were tired of waiting for this boy to come. We were looking forward to meeting him. The reduction was over. We had struggled with anxiety for what felt like a lifetime for this family. Now, we wanted to embrace the next phase of our lives—the phase of enjoying our children. We both held hope that having Noah would heal us. Maybe turn our bad feelings into good ones, start anew.

A day or two before Noah's birth, Jackie went for acupuncture to get things moving. The woman who gave the treatment told Jackie it would be about 24 hours until she would go into labor. About 12 hours later, she felt contractions, weak ones, but nevertheless, contractions. Off to see our midwives. It turned out that she was six centimeters dilated when we arrived at our appointment like she was with Maria. Jenna seemed disconnected and shy and I didn't like her energy. For example, she never remembered our names. We had started to love the midwives because of the older women that had been in charge, but Jenna was younger, and newer. Jenna did not represent the intuitive, wise, old crone energy that we wanted for this birth.

On the other side of our exam room wall, there was random

whispering. They knew from our last birth, that it could be 48 hours or more until we started active contractions. Plus, we didn't realize that Jenna was about to be off call, so a different midwife was going to have to help us birth Noah. They were discussing who should take over our birth if it crossed over the on-call start-end time. Sylvia was the midwife switching to the on-call midwife as we were nearing delivery. We LOVED Sylvia compared with all the other midwives. She grabbed both our hands as she greeted us in the exam room. She remembered us from months ago for a visit. Jackie and I both had an intuitive feeling that she would birth our baby. She had so much light around her. Confident, wise, grounded, fearless, Sylvia entered the room grinning and told us essentially that we had to get Jackie's water to break naturally in order to start having contractions. And if we wanted, we could go home and wait. Maria was with Jackie's mom, who prearranged to sleepover, so we had time. Jackie and I decided to discuss our thoughts.

Walking around the hospital in laps, we talked and talked about what to do and what we wanted for our future family. It was the best communication we'd had in months. We even laughed a little. After several hours of walking and debating whether we should go home that day, we decided to do more to get this baby out. He was very big and Jackie was uncomfortable. We went back into the hospital and asked Sylvia how to get the baby out today. They advised stripping her membranes to get her water to break. Bracing ourselves, putting her legs in the stirrups during contractions, Sylvia reached inside of my wife and got things moving. It's truly even more painful than it sounds "stripping membranes". Jackie was now in serious pain, but the point was to get the water to break.

She advised us to go freakin' walk again, so off we went, down the block to Square One for lunch in Holyoke. As I gazed down the street at the restaurant, it appeared miles away. "Stop worrying!" Jackie smiled as she waddled in moderate pain, but I couldn't stop. I don't like when I can't subdue or resolve pain. All I could think was, *Who wants to eat when there is a child hanging upside down between your legs?*

We sat at that table in that little luncheon, and tried to think of something besides contractions and big headed babies. I could feel that a larger life change was coming. Something good and something bad, like crossing into a new life realm. Not only our son was coming, but it was a strange, floaty sensation, like fear and excitement. "I feel a strange and ominous energy," Jackie admitted, looking at the floor.

"Yeah, so do I."

After lunch, walking back to the car was incredibly difficult for Jackie. She felt something trickling down her leg. It was blood. I was beginning to freak out. I wanted to sprint back to the birthing center and burn off all the energy in my body. "OK, I'm running to the car! You wait here!" I said, starting to walking backwards and jumping up and down once in a while.

"No! No! No! You are not leaving me here in Holyoke!" she yelled, waddling more quickly. "It feels so weird! It's like dropping down. It's almost like the baby is sliding down between my legs."

Fabulous, I thought. *We're walking in the middle of Holyoke, on the sidewalk, miles from help. What if she passes out? What if she falls?* I wished we had more support, family or friends, but we didn't. I wanted to call for help, but who?

The time and the waddling were all so slow and monotonous.

Luckily, we made it to the car, so we called Sylvia to meet us at the birthing center. Jackie was bleeding more steadily when we got there. And she was eight centimeters dilated, but still no strong contractions. The baby had a healthy heart rate. They kept examining her at the birthing center, debating. They finally decided to start Pitocin to intensify the contractions. Finally, she got her first real contractions with the help of drugs again to activate her uterus to squeeze. She lay there for about an hour and half, shaking and grunting and dilating more. Lynn was our Doula that day, she was new, but she was also Anya's friend and her Doula. She became our calming angel during this whole process.

Finally, Lynn decided to further help Noah out by putting Jackie in stirrups again. Lynn tipped the lip of the cervix to get the baby's head to move. That was 7:30 pm. Jackie began actively pushing around that time. I rubbed her back, always feeling somewhat useless. "Don't rub my back!" she would say. "I'm gonna puke!" she yelled. Birth is completely humiliating, because it's an enormous energy you must ride out without having any control or influence. It is sacred and fast moving, yet time also stops, flexing its power, its persistence. Watching the baby's head crown is odd and disgusting and blessed.

Moaning, yelling, hair, goop, blood, his face, Noah finally came out on March 21, 2010 at 9:05 pm, all 7 pounds and 14 ounces of him. His head was cone-shaped. His body was bulky!

Before they handed me Noah, I was at Jackie's bedside, with my hand on her head, Sylvia told her to push, and a large POP of blood burst out of her as she pushed out the placenta, then more blood flooding out behind it. Lynn quickly sat down to stop the bleeding,

Sylvia flanked her standing and looked strained. Lynn was sewing, but the bleeding was so much, she couldn't see. "Step aside, Lynn! Step aside!" Sylvia commanded loudly. Lynn grimaced and stood up and Sylvia plopped down in the chair fast to try to stop the bleeding.

A cloud formed in the room. No one was watching Noah in his crib, except me. Gradually, room noises began to echo in my head. People started running in and out of the room without strides, drifting. More people entered. The happy birth energy disintegrated. I overheard Sylvia calmly telling the nurse to call the doctor fast, then they fake-smiled at me and distracted me by handing me Noah all bundled up, warm and safe. He was so new and cute and sleepy. A long line of hopes and dreams in a cartoon bubble lined up over my head, one by one they entered my mind. We had waited for him. It took two years to create him. Tears were shed. There were four of us now. He was completely healthy. I might have to raise him alone. There was a downward pull, heaviness. Now, I had him in my arms and held him tight to my heart and held on for my life. He felt like a soft, hefty football. He was lumpy, sleeping and content, pink looking, eyes closed.

A gnawing feeling kept touching me, coolness. Jackie looked up at me from the tilted hospital bed about nine feet away. She looked much older, green and gray colored and they had her head down and her feet up. I froze there. Not moving towards her. She could see I started leaving. She reached her hand out to me and said "I don't want to die." It felt like a movie, where she was sliding away in the opposite direction as Noah and me, like a long hallway. Perspectives were changing. I was weak, almost faint. Coolness again touched me, then goosebumps. *She's dying*, I heard in my head. I focused on Noah, holding him closer to my chest. I thought it best to keep my eyes on him and pray. So I did.

I tried to drop all the anger in my heart towards Jackie. *Dear God, don't let her die!* What if she did die? I didn't want her to. Honesty swept over me. *It's true, I don't want her in my life, but someone else might make her happy. I don't love her, but someone else could.* She was bleeding out. She lost 650 mL of blood, her pressure had dropped to 66/40. I clearly remember Sylvia's strong, loud voice. She was sewing Jackie's torn uterus, at the same time, she sat up straight, looking over Jackie's pelvis to lock eyes and said loudly. "Jackie! Jackie, look at me!!!! Look at me!!" Jackie swerved her head, tried to pull up and met Sylvia's gaze. "You are fine! Your baby is fine! It is time for you to STOP bleeding!!!!" A chill ran through me with the words. She heard her! Intention is everything, and Sylvia had put intention into her demand. Sylvia had a will that was going to save Jackie. 'Not on my watch!' her tone said.

The conviction of her statement, her strength, and her determination were powerful in that moment. It rippled through the room and it reverberated in me. Finally, the doctor showed up and she reached inside Jackie to stop the bleeding as well. They kept apologizing to Jackie. Each time they reached in, Jackie screamed out and yelled in horrible pain. She passed out from the pain and blood loss but they successfully stopped the bleeding uterus. They saved her life while I clung to Noah and prayed.

The lining of her placenta had grown so large due to having been designed for three babies. It had ripped a hole in her uterus. They kept reaching inside of her and trying to get the uterus to clamp down and stop bleeding, but it hadn't worked, until Sylvia told her to stop

103

bleeding. She did stop bleeding. After an hour or so of Jackie recovering and receiving blood, she woke up and began to have color in her face again. One of the midwives held up the placenta for me to see it. It was utterly disgusting, yet miraculous. It was large enough to hold three Noah's!!! It was a very large, gray sheath stretching three feet wide and 18 inches tall, like skin, a bodily sac, or a see-through sleeping bag. The placenta still grew inside Jackie, holding a space for the two babies that never had the chance to be.

After the birth, withered and raw, Jackie and I whispered in the hospital bed about all that had happened, wondering how Maria was doing. The room felt empty and dim. "I'm glad I'm alive tonight," she said through tears, "I thought I was going to die. I feel like I'm being punished. I'm not sure I'll ever be forgiven for that difficult decision!" I simply cried. I didn't know what to say. I had my own guilt and resentment, for wanting those boys, but not fighting for them. We were two women who needed more than just one another. We needed support from many. We needed forgiveness. We longed for someone loving to soothe us and say, "There, there, all of life is still loving and fair. All those tough times are in the past." I was such a worried mess that evening once Jackie recovered from childbirth. All the anxiety in my body had showed up late to the birth, I never showed my anxiety during. No one could see it. I always looked extremely relaxed. It was like aftershock from holding it together for so long! But now my body shook and twitched. All of us were alive....plus one. Noah was content in his own little bed next to us in that dark birthing room.

Maria stayed with Jackie's mom that evening at our house. She was awake all night. It was the first time in her 4 ½ years without either Jackie or me there for her. When I brought her the next day to see Jackie and Noah at the birthing center, she was so excited to meet her little brother. Jackie's mom was there also. As I walked out of the hospital, Maria wept in my arms and all the way home. "Can I go to bed?" she asked. "Of course," I said. So I put her in bed to sleep at 3 pm in the afternoon. She was exhausted, emotionally and physically. She slept all afternoon and into the night until the next morning.

When Jackie and Noah got home from the birthing center, she was weak from blood loss. I had to take care of everyone now, all three of them. After three months, Jackie was fully recovered and we both went back to work. Striding through the door after returning from my first day of work, I was greeted by Jackie in the kitchen with, "Who have you been cheating on me with?"

"What? What are you talking about?" I frowned.

"Don't play innocent with me! Who are you seeing? You're obviously in love with her!"

It was like a bad movie. I hadn't ever cheated on Jackie. I had feelings, but never acted on them. I had crushes, but never acted on them. But I wrote about them.

"Did you read my journal?" I asked. I raised my voice. My stance on private writing was solid. As humans, we are allowed to vent and express our feelings in writing. I consider it sacred. "You have no right to read my journal. We just gave birth to a new baby and you almost died and now you are trying to push me away because of a journal that you should NOT be looking at!!!!"

I went on, "I always vent my feelings in my journal. I never cheated on you! When things get dark, you always make them deeper and darker. You have GOT to stop suffering and punishing yourself!!"

"If you don't want to hear about my feelings for other women, then I suggest you get your damn nose out of my journals!" I said with my fists clinched and shaking.

She slowly backed out of the room. She knew I was right. She was silenced. Is that what standing in your power feels like? I wanted more. We never discussed it again, not ever.

Stupid Stubborn

Stubborn is having or showing dogged determination
not to change one's attitude or position on something,
especially in spite of good arguments or reasons to do so.

Our fresh new family moved as a unit through the house, tethered together. Life with two kids was entirely different than only one. Each adult had one child to care for if we were together, which was rare. And when one of us left the house, the other parent was outnumbered by two kids. Both cried at the same instant. Both spoke over each other, even when Noah couldn't speak yet. Two sets of eyes hoping for attention from me all the time.

Maria was four and a half years old. She was an exceptionally excellent big sister who loved her little brother. She loved helping him, holding him, and loving with him. Sometimes she talked to him and paid better attention than his moms.

"Don't worry Noah," she chatted with him in a sweet high pitched voice, while I changed his diaper. Flat on his back, feet kicking around aimlessly in the air, he was staring at her mesmerized. She leaned over him and delivered this sentence,

"Don't worry Noah; your penis will get bigger as you get bigger!! Don't worry big guy. It will.......right Ma?"

"Yes Maria, it will."

Those little moments as a bystander were funny. Watching these two kids interact together was a blessing, but it seemed like Jackie wanted to keep me a bystander. Both children were Jackie's territory; her prized possessions. She trained Maria by now to do exactly as she asked. No one did it like she did it. With Maria sitting in the warm bath, Jackie timed exactly two minutes to leave conditioner in her hair. She was vigilant about her timing. Distracted by the laundry, Jackie went downstairs, so I blew off the exact timing of the cream rinse and told Maria to drain the tub. "You can dry off now," I told her. "Has it been two minutes?" Maria asked, worried. "Yes, it has" I answered not knowing or caring. She looked down at the water. Maria seemed aware that I was purposely breaking Jackie's rules.

So sweet, those moments after a bath, drying off meant cuddling into a towel, and Maria loved the one-on-one attention and affection, the smell of soap and lavender. We were giggling and enjoying each other, when Jackie came storming into the bathroom, her hands on her hips, "Did you put the conditioner in?" she asked.

"Yes," I said calmly, "We were done, so she got out."

She did not like that I cut her out of the bath deal, although, I was never sure why Jackie reacted. I could sense her anger but didn't know why.

"Did you leave it in for two full minutes?" she prodded.

"Yes," I lied. "No big deal."

That phrase triggered her. She flared. "Why do you have to talk to me like that???" her voice got louder.

"Don't Mama! Please don't fight!" Maria pleaded.

"Chill out!" I yelled back at Jackie! Why was she always angry? What did it matter if the conditioner was in for 1 minute or 3 seconds? I was pissed and defiant.

"What difference does it make?!?" My time connecting with Maria was more important than the damn cream rinse!

Jackie began to rant, almost yelling to herself, "Can you stop yelling at me and calm down and let me finish my sentences?" This was a common defense, claiming that I wasn't letting her finish her sentences. The fight kept escalating, and when Maria ran into her bedroom to escape the fighting, I followed her, slammed the door, and we held on to each other, footsteps behind us. She seemed to snap in a fury behind the closed door as it came between her and Maria. Bang! Bang! Bang! Her balled up fists hit the door. "Let me in there! Don't you hurt her!" she screeched. Her voice cracked in desperation. What was she talking about? Why was she so angry? I would never hurt her.

I eventually responded through the door, "Not until you calm down!" I was proud to stand up to Jackie. I hugged Maria close, smelling conditioner. Jackie's banging got more rapid, and I could hear her cursing. The door was never locked. Because Jackie sounded to be getting worse, I opened the door, "Don't you hurt her!" she rushed through the threshold in tears, moving towards Maria, arms outstretched.

Dumbfounded, I didn't budge. What was she referring to? Was she losing her mind? I looked at Jackie. "What? Why would I hurt her? You're the one flipping out. I didn't say anything!" "But you called her a 'piece of shit.' I heard you!" she said, starting to cry.

"No, I did not!" I looked at her in disbelief and opened my arms wide to show I had nothing to hide.

It all blew up so fast. And then we didn't know what to say to one another. It hadn't made any sense, only pure dark emotions. Jackie seemed to have the feelings first and then create a drama to provide stories for her fits of anger. She calmed down and cried, holding Maria who kept her eyes on me. Maybe, she felt she had to protect Maria from me, but I wasn't hurting her. In fact, I'd thought I was protecting Maria from Jackie. This was the first time I noticed Jackie's projection. Would Jackie harm my kids? There's always that instinct to protect your kids, just in case, even against your spouse. I usually trusted Jackie, yet I doubted her now. How the hell did we get here? Her reality was 'off.'

Now she was scaring me. God knows I wanted to leave my marriage and my situation or change it, but leaving still seemed impossible for me. I hated confronting her, anything to avoid her huge feelings. Making decisions was heartache for me, especially if it went against the will of Jackie. Disagreeing with Jackie was freakin' courageous! Yet, she was getting more violent after that episode, like leaving was unavoidable. Plus I was more afraid of her after that episode. Motorcycles drove by our house with loud, cracking engines several times a day and at night and Jackie blinked the porch lights and ran out the door and yelled at them from the sidewalk like an angry dog because she was trying to get the kids to sleep. One time, I stood up to Jackie and told her about my thoughts on homeschooling when she immediately grabbed Maria out of her bedroom in the evening and said, "We're leaving! I don't need to listen to your shit!"

She pulled Maria out of bed, put shoes on her and jumped in the car with Maria to run away from me. I walked outside and told her to come in. Maria was scared, so Jackie came back inside the house with no further discussion.

Thank God they did, because her threat cut deep in my heart. I never brought it up again. I had convinced myself early on that Jackie was logical and sensible, but in reality, she revealed that she was becoming more and more emotional and reactive and threatening. I now considered her insane and unreasonable, particularly towards me. If I ended this, our separation and divorce would not be easy. I was required to stand in my power because she was unpredictable and worst of all, unfair.

Maria began to see the difference between Jackie and me as parents. She started using them to her advantage. For example, with me, Maria was allowed to miss dance lessons sometimes or not eat all her vegetables or veer off the routine. To combat this pattern, Jackie took over. As Maria got closer to five years old, Jackie suggested, "Maybe I should bring Maria to her ballet lesson, you have trouble getting her to do anything."

I wasn't allowed to drop Maria off because one time she decided not to go to class. So Jackie cut me out of event after event because I wasn't forcing Maria to attend every time. Rigidity. Maria capitalized on any change in routine, which is what I offered. I liked choices as a child, so I gave choices to my child. "You're not consistent! Maria needs structure!" Jackie yelled at me. No change EVER was Jackie's consistent way.

She tried to anticipate my shortcomings, which made me feel like I was filled with shortcomings. If Noah took a nap too late, it was my fault that he wouldn't fall asleep at night. Or I must have given him too much sugar before bed. If I made a mistake in the checkbook, she took over paying all the bills. If Maria's hands got sore or red, I used the wrong soap. It was always my fault. I was the other parent in the house working against her. After a while, I was considered the wrong one, but I still preferred being right, so I kept trying. I became more organized. I grew timelier. My parenting skills got better as the kids grew up.

Maria snarked at me, "Ma, you're always late for everything! Why are you so late all the time?" The kid couldn't even tell time yet, but she could repeat Jackie's message of my fictitious deficiencies as a mom. I'm no later to events than anyone. In fact, when I began timing myself, I was timelier than most people, particularly Jackie. My child began to blame me and belittle me just as it was modeled to her. This was not going to happen! I thought to myself. I need my kids to see the real me, NOT the parent that was low man on the totem pole, not the person Jackie labeled me. Not the mouse, not the slave, not the doormat, I was determined not to be treated like a child in this family. I was determined to maintain my kind nature. Maria and Noah needed me to grow up and stand in my power fast! I wrote in my poem when she was feeling sick, "It hurts to be so close to Maria, and it hurts to keep myself so far away." I didn't feel worthy or capable, yet I kept my love at a distance. None of Jackie's insults towards me would have worked if I hadn't believed it to some degree. Somewhere I thought I wasn't good enough. They needed two parents. It was time to have a voice.

Around six, I began to worry about Maria. She started spending too much time making her bed. Before getting into bed for the night, she slowly stripped the bed sheets and comforter off and then began to rebuild it. She smoothed out the sheet, and then smoothed it out again and then tucked in all the excess sheets under the mattress tight, so the wrinkles were gone. "What are you doing?" I stood and watched her. "I have to get all the wrinkles out." She said moving around the bed. "Why?" I asked her. "Because it needs to be perfect! I need all the wrinkles out before I get into the bed!" She went to each corner of the bed and pulled it taut. She was methodical. It worried me. I worried about her compulsiveness, the perfection of her behavior. I noticed her doing it the next week also, but she did it longer and was getting upset when the wrinkles kept showing up. It was useless because once she got into bed, the wrinkles came back. I wondered why she was doing it. Jackie made hospital corners from being in the military. Could Maria have gotten yelled at for wrinkling the sheets while Jackie made the bed? Was Maria copying behavior she saw in Jackie? Was it control? Did she need some say over her Fate, and the wrinkles eased her mind when she removed them? Did I do something to make her this way?

I recalled bedtimes when Maria was younger, times with us playing more. I held her pajama bottoms, and she bounced on the bed. She jumped as high as possible into her pajama bottoms. She loved it and giggled and laughed every night with me. But now, here she was stressed and smoothing out the sheets over and over and over again. What happened?

It was the same with Maria's hair. Another tense brawl, every morning, was when Jackie brushed out the knots in Maria's hair, and then pulled it back so tight that it was flat to her head like she was bald. Her hair perfectly molded to the shape of her head. Between the

113

hair brushing, Jackie's bitching about it, plus Maria's crying, it was like a self-induced drama. Maria cried that it hurt, but eventually, she began checking it in the mirror and yelling at Jackie for not doing it "right." "It's sticking up!" She yelled. "Do it again!" Jackie used to tell me stories of her childhood suffering because her mom hurt her by brushing too roughly; now, she was doing the same thing to Maria. Why couldn't Jackie stop the pattern?

As Maria pulled her hair tie out, Jackie locked horns with her. "Maria! This is the last time!" but Maria only pulled it back out again. Jackie did as Maria asked, yet screamed at her also. Maria was creating a pattern, but no one could stop it. Jackie let her do it over and over again. Neither of them could just let her hair down. Both of them were becoming a slave to the perfection of Maria's ponytail.

On the mornings I had to do her hair, Maria directed me more than she did Jackie, but there was a huge problem. Each time I pulled her hair back and tied it, Maria asked for it to be tighter, getting more and more frustrated, just like Jackie did. Eventually, she jumped out of her chair telling me, "You're not doing it right! Do it again! Do it again!" After the fourth time, I said no more. "No, honey, I did it already. You keep pulling it out. I can't do it perfectly. I can't do it tighter."

That's when she lost it. She began sobbing and writhing around on the floor. "Please, Ma! Do it perfect! Do it again! You're not doing it right; I can see the hair sticking up! I need it flat to my head!"

I kept saying, "You're OK, Maria! You're OK!" but no words helped—she couldn't be consoled. She needed me to be certain and strong and solid, but I got drenched in her feelings. I had a sinking feeling inside watching her struggle and fight over what was "nothing." I couldn't save her, and it killed me. I fell apart too. My feelings grew as big as hers. "I Can't! I Can't! I Can't!" I repeated it out loud over and over and over, slowly, slowly letting out the steam of my anger. I truly was helpless. After that terrible tantrum, I never was allowed by Jackie or Maria to do her hair again. Eventually, the fights between Jackie and Maria became worse and worse over her hair, over what she wore, over what she ate. And everyone heard about how hard it was for Jackie to deal with such an ungrateful child, an impossible child. "See what I have to deal with?" Not until Maria was shamed. Finally, Jackie taught Maria to do her own hair and pull it back herself and wet it down to her head if it's not entirely flat. Any hair sticking up made Maria want to begin again brushing.

We were screwing up our kid. I couldn't do this. A child's struggle is a barometer for their parent's emotional health. What must it feel like for Maria? There's a palpable stress inside her, an audible cry. The sheets and her hair, both viewable "tells" of her struggles, which were OUR struggles. The visible strain between two moms played out in a child who deserves more deserves love. This motivated me to try to find a solution with Jackie. Talk to her…or something. I had to do something!

That night, I asked Jackie, "Are you happy?"

"Yes," she answered immediately. "Yes, I'm very happy."

I thought, *How could you be happy? Denial will not encourage growth and change. Why would she ever choose change if she thought our lives were happy now?* I was not happy, but I never honestly admitted it. Maria wasn't thriving either. Noah was too little yet. My definition of happiness was joy and laughter and freedom and fun and, most of all, love. I didn't feel any of those daily or weekly, and I kept blaming Jackie.

Both of us each had our own therapists early on in our relationship, but now the money was tight with two kids. Jackie and I had gone to couples therapy for about seven years of our ten years together before kids, but nothing changed or improved. Each week we tried to change our behaviors and find quality time together as a couple, but it was rare. We didn't have a weekly date night. We didn't get a babysitter until Noah was one. Neither of us liked leaving our kids with other people. Jackie seemed to book all our free time visiting her family in Connecticut every weekend, whether she enjoyed her family or not. During the week, we seemed to fall back into our usual habits as a couple quickly. Our roles were like ruts we couldn't roll out of. She blamed me for everything bad, and she made decisions for everyone. I lived in the present, she planned for the future. I was too flexible. She was too rigid. The therapist suggested we try to switch roles, but we never did.

To deal with her negative energy and my own sadness, I used music. I began humming and playing guitar whenever she was around me. I took guitar lessons to feel better. It made me lighter and stopped my mind from worries. I've never hummed before, yet when she was close to me, I hummed to separate myself from her energy, to lift me up. Jackie hated noise near her, so I played guitar out in the toy room with the door closed. It was quiet and away from everyone. I needed to get away. I wished she liked my playing, but she didn't. So alone, I sipped red wine, wrote poetry, and strummed my guitar on cold winter nights.

But she wanted my attention more than I could offer it. Alone time was my daydreaming and "spacing out" time. She tried to glom on to me. Either she wanted my help moving something or fixing the computer or cleaning something. Soothing my worries and doubts were part of my practice, my habits, I started to need time to myself. She thought the dishes were more important than her own peace of mind. I couldn't be around all that self-sacrificing! I needed to save myself in any small step I could. Eventually, if she came into the room, I left the room. When she arrived, I departed. Two separate souls in the same house.

Since Jackie didn't think there was a problem, and since couples' therapy hadn't been useful for us, I went to see a psychic for a better perspective. I wondered what my future looked like. Her name was Iva. She was a teacher and an energy worker who studied Christianity and spirituality for over 30 years. A friend from work used her every six months to guide her through her upcoming life events. "Hello, my Dear." She said kindly, with her strong Polish accent, then hugged me. She was intelligent and loving; a teddy bear. Iva wore thick glasses and had a thick belief system.

We sat in the basement of her home, in a small dim room with photos of Jesus on the walls. She knew numerology and pulled cards from two different decks, one tarot, and one traditional playing cards. Date of birth was the one detail I told Iva about my family and me. She wrote the numbers down and scratched out some patterns connecting the numbers. My goal was to get guidance for leaving Jackie somehow. Perhaps leaving Jackie would make things better for all of us. My heart ached with concern for my kids and their future. She smiled and said, "You are ready to leave, huh? Yes? Jackie is stupid stubborn."

She told me about Jackie as if I didn't know, "She is a good Mama, but she is stubborn to a fault, stupid stubborn." She showed me three kings in her hand. "Who are the three boys?" she asked only minutes after I sat down. Tears poured down my face. "These are the boys we were pregnant with recently. We had to eliminate two of them. They were triplets. My son was one of three."

"Do NOT think about it or regret it!" she said loudly, waving her hand in the air. "It is over! It is done! No regrets! How it turned out is how it was MEANT to be!" Iva told me Noah would like animals and love everything and have a lot of wavy brown hair. "You are blessed with your two beautiful, healthy children," she said.

She talked fast and knew many things about my personality and my family. She said she reads auras and energy. She told me to take care of myself by focusing on being in nature and writing often. Looking at her cards and flipping them over, she casually said, "Jackie throws her emotions on you, huh? Don't absorb it! Don't drink zee poison!" Her guidance was very comforting, "Your kids will be OK. They love you both very much. You will teach them about this world, and they will teach you too." She then said something I hadn't heard before from any human. "You are a loving mom! Your kids truly love you! You are more special than you believe. You are a very powerful person!"

This was another time I let in the light of my kids' love. I acknowledged that maybe I was a good Ma, perhaps I did deserve Love. Tears in my eyes, I opened up my beliefs to more possibilities. More love in my life from my kids and more supportive people. Iva opened my eyes to the larger picture, to the critical connection between my kids and me. I wasn't only devoted to Jackie anymore; I had children now! They needed me. And I needed them too. Maybe I could create a new loving space with these two new kiddos in my life.

Sand Away the Cuts

Cuts are openings, incisions, or wounds
in something caused with a sharp-edged tool or object.

As much as I adored my children, as much as I wanted to avoid stress in my life, I still found myself counting my potential losses, rather than my blessings. Incessant agenda in my head made me a jagged form of myself. Kids on my hip, in their cute overalls, saying sweet sentences weren't penetrating my miserable me-thoughts. There was a vicious voice in my head, the grump, the inner critic! I blamed everything around me, especially Jackie. Life was cruelly happening to me. The ideas and labels in my mind for what could be best for my kids and my family weren't manifesting. I was blocked and stifled by Jackie's demands and my constant inner crank.

One particular sticking point between her and me was the effort and cost of homeschooling. I was stressed about the cost of now sending two kids to a homeschooling program at private school prices. I was also stressed they were growing older and spending too much time with only me and Jackie.

Originally, Maria was so shy and strained in groups, we decided to homeschool. She froze around other children. It took her over an hour to warm up at gatherings with other families. We took her to see the smaller charter school her friends were attending, and she told us "No way do I want to be around all those kids!" when she was 6. We kept her home instead. A fraction of me agreed, but Noah loved socializing. He smiled nonstop at other kids and other people. He loved charming people, babbling, leaning out of my arms to touch, kiss, or smile at strangers at five months old. Learning about *everything,* he thrived in the outdoor Arcadia preschool. Jackie was adamant that we should homeschool both children. I hoped she would change her mind after he attended Arcadia with such ease, but changing her decisions was unseen thus far.

One afternoon, I approached the subject with Jackie. We sat together reading at the kitchen island when I admitted, "I don't think Noah needs to be homeschooled! And I'm not sure we should homeschool Maria anymore. It costs so much more than sending them to school. We may not be able to afford these alternative programs like Arcadia. It's like paying for private school. It seems silly to recruit our educator to instruct privately for Noah and 5 or 6 additional homeschooling students. Are you sure the public schools aren't a good option for us?" It took a community to raise kids, and as it was, we had no help, and little money, always in debt, always using our bank's overdraft protection loan. We couldn't even afford a babysitter. "What about school? We pay taxes. Are you sure the schools in our area are bad?" I asked her, hoping for a discussion. Hoping to hear her thoughts, Jackie turned and looked at me in all seriousness and said

"Who do you think knows more about kids? Me? Or You?" There were no words....I wanted to punch her in the face with all my strength. Instead, I said, "But I'm asking you a reasonable question. Are the schools in our community really bad or what?"

She blinked at me with big eyes and then said, "We are a homeschooling family! I see kids every day at work! They all hate school! There is no kid currently in our public school systems that enjoy school anymore! It's not like it was when you and I went to school! That's why we are a homeschooling family! It's a *lifestyle*!" "But how will we ever know if we never go and never let our kids go?" I asked calmly. Her eyes got fiery, and her shoulders got higher to be bigger and more convincing, "I'm not sending my kids to a public school!! Maria is sensitive, and she needs to be homeschooled. I want to be the influence in her life, not her friends and popular culture! That's why we are a homeschooling *family*!"

So we homeschooled, which meant day trips as field trips, museums and side programs with other homeschooled families, all at a cost, even it was parking and cost of admissions, still much more money than being in school from 8 to 3 pm. What would public school cost? Couldn't we try it? Would my kids ever be exposed to public school? Would they ever ride a school bus, join a team, be in a club, or participate in parades?

Fortunately, homeschool kids are allowed to participate in many of these after-school activities and recreation leagues, but their friends weren't in those programs. Maria joined recreational basketball for three seasons in a row, but none of the kids knew her. She made a friend sometimes, but they only saw each other once per week playing basketball. It still wasn't the same as being around peers daily. Many of the girls already paired up with their friends from public school. There were three homeschooling groups, but again, Maria never found connections because she didn't see them regularly, only weekly. Her first group of friends at the age of two, all split up and went to different types of kindergarten programs, but none of them homeschooled except Maria. I didn't feel we were helping her social weaknesses.

Not only did I want them to try public school, but I also hated our homeschooling lifestyle. Our daily set-up was painful to me. Every other day one of us was alone with the kids. I hadn't intended on raising my kids alone or independently for 12 hours, three days a week. I had expected help—*lots* of help from Jackie, but also from teachers, babysitters, friends or playdates. Nothing I did was gathering help. I was socially shy and reserved. I didn't make friends easily, so I wasn't building a community at all. Eventually we hired a babysitter to watch Maria at home while I telecommuted, but naturally, she came to whatever room I was in to find me or interrupt or cry. I would tell her to stay with the babysitter, but she didn't. I was the rope in the tug of war between myself and each child and my wife and my dog. Pulling and pulling, each one barking needs at me. It was stretching me out. 7 am with kids until 7 pm when Jackie came home; then I worked until midnight afterward. Not conducive to quality work. Then I was awake early to leave at 7 the next morning for my hour or more commute to work until 5:30 pm and drive home another hour, depending on traffic. I was living in someone else's set of rules. It was my life, but I was living in Jackie's plan, Jackie's routine, Jackie's space, Jackie's ideas, Jackie's parenting style, Jackie's everything. Not conducive to a quality marriage. Every other day involved hours with kids, hours I needed to be alone, to sneak away, to rejuvenate. Alone time is what I required to act civilized and not so damn grumpy.

When I finally took some time, it wasn't mine. "What are you doing?" she'd say as I innocently did step aerobics in the living room in front of *Will and Grace.* "I'm exercising." I'd say. "Really? Exercising? When there's so much shit to do to get ready for tomorrow!" she'd explode at me. "I'll help with everything, but first I'll work out." I calmly reasoned. Hearing that, she began to cry. She seemed exhausted. I kept making adjustments to help Jackie try to be happier and more comfortable, deep down drowning in my self-analysis and anxiety. Every action was to avoid her reaction. Slowly, in those evenings, I closed down my heart and went far away, invisible. I told myself it was all fine, praying for my sense of humor to save me from all the blaming and numbing out. I was holding tight that my issues were acceptable and reasonable. Hoping any deep-seated conflicts or causes would slowly fade away. Instead, our emotions and our disagreements were growing rapidly worse.

Noah was three and Maria was seven by now. I often felt I couldn't give all my attention to my telecommuting work at the same time as giving my children quality stimulation and educational activities and love. Parenting felt too competitive. Parents like Jackie were doing many different activities to keep their kids educated and advancing. I was a subpar parent! I began to crack. Working on my laptop until eleven every other evening because my telecommuting time was spent with the kids, was tearing me into pieces. Between my kids and my work obligations, I was split, failing to be present. The iPhone and emails were a curse. Each message disrupted my day with my kids and put me on high alert to not disappoint my supervisors' research. It was a "lose-lose" situation. Either I was guilty for not putting in my hours toward work or guilty for missing my kids' special life moments.

Normally, Jackie walked through the door after work, coat still on, and asked, "Did you get to return the library books?" or "Did you clean the bathroom?" or "Did you fix the cabinet?" or "Did Maria do the worksheet I left out for her to complete?" *On my workday??????* I always hoped to hear, "Hello, how was your day?" Instead, her expectations were hurtful, unloving, fueling my anger. When she arrived home, her disappointment in me was loudly banging around in my conscience. Teach the kids, love the kids, spend 12 hours with the kids, clean the house, make the dinner, and oh yes, work full time. I sipped wine at 11 am on some days to soothe my anger and anxiety. *How could I do this again?* I stressed myself out, and I stressed the kids as we got closer to Jackie's arrival. I hadn't realized I was doing it. Each morning started relaxed, but as time drained away, so did my comfort. Picking up, cooking, and paying attention to them pulled me apart. After 5 pm was the worst time for me to be cranky and on edge because the kids were cranky too! And hungry!!

One typical Thursday with my stay-at-home kids, it was 6 pm, and I was trying to get them to pick up their toys. Noah was rapidly pulling everything off the shelves that I had carefully put back in its place, only seconds before. Maria was moving furniture to the sides of the room to make space to do more leaps or dances or tumbling. The house was utterly rearranged, no floor to be seen!!

This particular evening, my wide goblet of red wine was not relaxing me enough. At times, wine helped me be more playful with the kids, and it helped my strain feel lesser on all of us. But today, the clock ticked heavy in my ears. My dog, Sienna constantly barked at me to feed her or give her treats. As the pork chops sautéed on the stovetop, I calmly asked my kids to clean up the toys, as I flipped the chops with a spatula. "Start picking up please." No one moved at my request. They kept playing. Passing through the living room, the smell of garlic and butter in the air, I asked nicely again and was nicely ignored by the little ones who had no idea my last nerve was rubbed as the clock ticked. My voice rose louder. "Pick Up!!" I started grabbing toys and throwing them. One smashed against the TV. Maria screamed. The TV was bleeding, colors dripping down the center. That's when I finally felt their gazes on me; I was snapping. Adrenaline fueled me, picking up speed. I loosened my lid, holding back all that emotion all day, a pressure cooker of anger. My kids quickly dropped their dolls; they changed from ignoring me to eyes locked on me, steady, looking fearful. I had their attention, undivided. The power of being heard engulfed me. Everything stopped. Quickly, my slide from my parental power slipped from my clutches into crazy town. In slow motion, I grabbed a knife out of the butcher's block to accentuate my words. The knife was banging on the chair in sync with my commands, so they might listen to each syllable as I spoke them loudly and deliberately, repeating. "Pick up, pick up, pick up, when I ask you to pick up your toys!" The feel of the knife sinking into the softwood relieved me. It sunk into me that my kids' fear was motivating them to look at me, the cuts in the chair showed my lack of control. Suddenly, the terror in their innocent eyes registered on my heart. I came back to my body, sobered up, ran to the sink, and dropped the knife in the dirty dishes. None of us will ever forget that moment. I apologized and cried, face in my hands. "I need you guys to listen to me better," I said under my breath. They unfroze and went back to playing, drama over. That night, I didn't mention anything to Jackie at first. I tried to sand away the cuts, but they were scarred, not only in the chair but into my kids and me.

This behavior was not normal. Not for me. It was my wake up call, my rock bottom. Only I could help me. Only I was seeing or listening to my daily struggles, my inner critic, my negativity. No one was rescuing me. No one knew.

To others, Jackie was easy to talk to, giggling, and charming in her circle of friends. I certainly couldn't complain about Jackie, or admit that I was failing at marriage and failing at parenting. I was so stuck. I wanted to hide. I loathed myself. It didn't reflect well on me to complain about my wife! At this same time, a co-worker of mine had just lost her sister to domestic homicide. Her brother-in-law, no prior incidents, had simply stabbed her sister 749 times. Why? What happened? Who does such a thing? Was I capable of murder? In the evening, after the knife in the chair incident, I stepped closer to the back door, nose almost touching the glass, looking out the window at my yard, praying. I saw my reflection in the pane. "What should I do?" I asked the universe. My own eyes close up looked back. I was honestly alone in this struggle, pretending my support was coming from Jackie. I had to solve my misery. No more blaming or whining. No more excuses! I needed to help myself to help my kids. Nothing was working; not therapy, not medication, not exercise, not a vacation, not talking with Jackie. Nothing ever changed—yet.

Part 4: Healing

Healing is the process of making or becoming
sound/whole or healthy again.

Their Mere Presence

Presence is the state or fact of existing,

occurring, or being present in a place or thing.

Sitting on a stool in my kitchen, my friend Ned faced me, smiled softly, and said, "You look gray. Are you okay?"

I blinked, heavy, embarrassed. He felt sorry for me. I was ashamed, my suffering and unhappiness showed on my face. I was feeling like a bad mom. Our kids were playing outside together. My self-sacrificing home life showed, and it was killing me. He lifted his necklace over his head and leaned over me to put it around my neck; a very kind, simple act. He said it would help raise my energy up, pull my vibration higher. It was a copper ring. It did have a soft, strange vibrational buzz to it. More importantly, the act of him "seeing" me plus recognizing and acknowledging my despair seemed to shift something within me—like an opening-up, rather than a closed-off, defensive feeling. I was more vulnerable as if I were showing my weaknesses. I was grateful to him. Ned was the first parent to talk with me. As a non-biological lesbian mom, I had moments of not fitting in with other parents. At gatherings, dads were in one corner bonding and moms in another. Where did I belong? The men didn't feel comfortable with me, often excluding me. The women were bonding with Jackie about breastfeeding or other types of conversations to which I couldn't relate. Plus, I wanted to give her space to socialize and vent without me next to her. In general, I enjoyed talking with men much more than women, but most of the dads had tight-knit friendships.

But Ned was the one person who noticed me and approached me first. Then, out of the kindness of his heart, he handed me his necklace. It was the first time I started to trust a friend to help me. I know I had been isolating myself and scared to reach outside my relationship. There were a few other dads I tried to ask to grab a beer and talk, but they usually declined my offers. Ned was the first friend I let in. We talked about energy and raising kids. He said, "Sometimes just the intention of hoping your child doesn't get hurt can make you exhausted. We can get depleted from so much worry." I let him help me by admitting my struggles. Such a small act of kindness like listening and sharing had a huge impact on my life.

A few weeks later, Ned reached out again to offer me "a reading." In a text, he said giving me his necklace opened him and altered him in a very positive way. I agreed that something good shifted from that kind act of sharing his necklace. Ned seemed to believe in things he couldn't see, such as energy and intentions. So did I—sort of. I must have shown a little bit of interest. I guess that's why he asked if I wanted "a reading."

Ned was studying under William Curtain, Ph.D., to be a

medical intuitive. Dr. Curtain is a Doctor of Ministry in Psychology. I had no idea what "a reading" involved. I didn't study energy medicine, but I had heard of it. I was intrigued. I only believed in nature or some greater power. I was very open to trying new things. So I said "yes"!

I left my cubicle at work to text with Ned. Over the phone texting, Ned explained to me what "a reading" from a Medical Intuitive involved on my part and his part. Ned's part is that he "channels." Almost embarrassed, Ned explained, "You can ask the universe a question or two, using me as the medium to interpret the answers"....odd, I thought, but "yes, OK." I landed on two questions to ask the universe. So I texted two short sentences from my desk at work for the universe to potentially answer. "Does the woman I have a crush on feel the same about me?" and "What can I do to heal my sore skin?"

Those seem like strange questions, but I had been "crushing" and obsessing on this one woman at work for almost five years. That's a long time to attempt to befriend someone who's entirely not interested in knowing you, pathetic and draining also. She had chosen to remain professional and not be friends. She eventually cut all communication with me. I guessed I wasn't supposed to have a relationship with her. Although I didn't want to cheat on Jackie, I honestly was interested in pursuing some sort of connection with her. I was sure that I needed to lead myself into some other life change because of this woman.

Stella was my physical therapist at work. My shoulder began making my arm go numb. I couldn't mouse at my desk without pain or numbness. In our weekly therapy sessions, we were utterly professional, but because there was touch involved during stretches and assessments, so a natural energy came through her hands to me. In fact, I liked the invisible line draw between us. It allowed me to be more open with her, not a friend, but not a colleague. I had more room to be authentic because I didn't see her anywhere outside of these appointments.

"Does your daughter believe in Santa Claus?" she asked me to make conversation.

"Oh yes!" I'd sit with my back to her and smile and share a story about Maria as she shared stories of her kids while working on my shoulder and neck.

"I'm worried my son is going to spoil it for my daughter who's older!" she laughed. Talking with her was easy. I was comfortable, yet innocent.

Once in the weight room, I called her over to ask her a question. As she was striding up to me, her energy swept over me like a wave, and a tingling sensation washed through me as she stopped to assess my wrist or hand. We "bumped" against each other energetically. Though it was purely my intuition and sensations that made me aware of any chemistry between us, I hadn't felt that crashing into someone in years. In the end, my wrist and shoulder healed and my weeks of physical therapy stopped. I emailed and called her a few times over several years to get together, but she grew annoyed. She told me not to call her anymore—she was working.

To release any feelings I had developed for her, I kept venting and smoldering in my journals about Love and Connection. I referred to Stella as my catalyst. Her acts of kindness combined with mine caused our natural chemistry to awaken a piece of me that I had completely shut down and cut off: my heart, my passion. She woke up an emotion inside me that I had forgotten about. The chemistry felt so vital to my life. So it was an excellent question to ask the universe why I was drawn to know her. Also, I was so disappointed in my marriage. I was empty inside. Daily, I blamed myself and my marriage for much of my sadness. And asking the universe if Stella liked me was hopeful.

My second question was about my sore skin. I had been picking my skin for more than 30 years. It had gotten worse in my marriage. I tried everything from behavior modification to dermatologists and was thinking of going to get plastic surgery. Again, this question was very important to me, because I had struggled with picking daily. I pick my face, especially when I'm stressed. And most of the time I can't stop myself. Standing in the mirror, I'm self-loathing, judging myself and trying to hide my flaws by picking. I've been doing it since I was a teenager, similar to cutting, it was a way to inflict pain on myself plus make me feel alive. I hoped it would clear up in my 40s. My skin only got worse as life got more stressful. My sores grow beneath the skin deep enough to hurt and create pressure, but they wouldn't pop or form whiteheads, they just hurt and looked ugly and swollen. I looked at everyone's skin and wonder if I would ever have smooth skin again. Eventually, the bump enticed me to squeeze it or touch it or pop, which made it get worse and sorer. Once, at four years old, Maria saw an old photo of me at 25. She said, "That picture doesn't look like you, because there's no spots. You have spots all over your face, Ma."

The evening after I sent the text, Ned met with his teacher and went into a sort of meditation/trance to "channel." The teacher asked Ned my two questions during Ned's trance state. Since it was a recorded session with his teacher, Ned took a long time to transcribe it on paper for me. It's not every day that the universe conveys messages to you. My patience was wearing thin. It wasn't until about 2 to 3 weeks later that I finally had answers that Ned had channeled that evening. Below was recorded in response to my two questions. Ned represents something omnipotent or loving, like Mother Nature or the Universe in this conversation. The teacher is trying to be vague to allow diverse concepts to be shared.

Ned: Alison has been losing focus.

Teacher: Alison is losing focus?

Ned: Yes. The focus has to do with her heart.

Teacher: Do you see her as having a physical heart problem?

Ned: No, we are speaking energetically.

Teacher: The emotional heart, a kind of diversification of her love interests?

Ned: No, we are talking about her current path. She is learning to open her heart and discover how to use it. There is a great deal of fear associated with her, this seems safe, this other person.

Teacher: Not so many risks or growth opportunities? Is that what you're saying? The other person seems safe?

Ned: [Safe] to the heart, and the feelings, both energetically and emotionally, parallel each other when she imagines herself opening herself energetically from the heart. She confuses this with the emotional attraction to this other person. There is a value to this emotion with this other person. If she believes to learn from this relationship, er, no, if she believes there is love, she needs to open her heart to her children. Because they are *authentic*, they will teach her whether the emotions she feels for this other person are what she believes they are. Because it is the clarity of the child that is pure and not judgmental. The learning she gets from this experience whether it be used for this other person or all those around her, this experience with the children is what she needs.

Teacher: They will teach her?

Ned: They will.

Teacher: The opening of the heart?

Ned: By their mere presence. But she has fear around that as well.

Teacher: What does she fear?

Ned: They will see her for who she is—her doubts—but as she learns to open her heart and be raw around them, she will come to understand the love that will guide her wherever she may go. That is all for that.

Teacher: Are skin issues not as important as her relationship issues?

Ned: They are merely part of it all.

Teacher: The skin issues are part of her?

Ned: It's her attempting to keep everything inside. The fear and doubt and uncertainty are bubbling out. When she opens her heart and allows herself to be authentic, be who she feels she is, there will be no need for these things to be trapped; it's an internal antidote for what is bubbling out of her skin.

Teacher: Thank you. That ties it all together.

This reading was a pivotal moment in my life. The weight of those words was fitting, tailored to me, inspiring. I carried the reading in my wallet for months. I read it over and over again. It was one of the first times I sensed something omnipotent and benevolent communicated to me directly. It gave me hope. Hope that things would work out for the best. Hope that I'm not in control of all of it. Hope that there is some unseen support. Every word resonated. "It is the clarity of the child that is pure and not judgmental." The kind of place I was living didn't involve love; it was judgmental; my judgment, as well as everyone else's. Struggling to be a parent, I realized I was avoiding love, avoiding loving my kids. I was afraid of loving myself. In my life experiences, love meant pain or betrayal or withdraw of love. If I opened my heart, then it was more vulnerable to being stabbed or abused. Or worse, I left yourself open to manipulation and punishment if I felt love and allowed a real connection. It was too risky, but not anymore.

Between Jackie and me, neither of us was expressing love to one another, and we were judging each other's parenting skills. I wanted more, something different. Ned's reading gave me hope; hope I could learn to love myself and others purely without judgment. Maybe I could open my heart again to love or learn to love with the help of my kids. I hoped to give and receive love unconditionally. My children would teach me, by their mere presence.

Shamanic Healings

Shamanic practitioners call on helping spirits in
unseen worlds to heal people here
by restoring their spiritual power.

At work that same week, I grew more honest with my friends about my frustrating relationship with Jackie. I didn't joke around as much at the lunch table; now, I complained for real.

"Jackie's been such a grumpy jerk lately," I shared. "The other day, she couldn't get Maria to go upstairs, so she just picked her up and threw her over her shoulder and carried her up, all angry. I was so pissed! I wanted to save Maria, but I was helpless to stop Jackie. I'm tired of all the hollering and fighting in my house. Jackie's such a rigid, control freak!"

Jade, one of my coworkers who heard me complain, carefully asked if I wanted to be one of her subjects to receive Shamanic healings. "I'm training to be a Shamanic healer. I recently had a friend drop out, so I have space for one more if you want. Greta and Steven are doing it too." She offered. "What do I have to do?" I asked worriedly. "You lay on a massage table, and I give you energy." She said, "I'll talk to the unseen world and try to answer questions for you. Help guide you in whatever aspect of your life you want to work on." Intrigued, I said "Sure!"

At our first meeting, Jade sat me down in her living room and explained to me what our very first session would look like together. She began by educating me.

"A Shaman is defined as a 'spiritual healer' and dates back thousands of years. Shamanism has been practiced on nearly all seven continents around the world. They were the spiritual healers of many different indigenous cultures."

"But what are you actually going to do?" I asked, worried.

"First, before you even arrive, I listen to a drum and go into a trancelike state and ask the unseen world *if* I can help you and *how* I can help you. I ask simple questions, and they guide me. Several different techniques can be used to heal you, but the session is commonly referred to as a Shamanic healing. In general, it's a way to restore and heal your body and your spirit back to wholeness. By using different Shamanic techniques, I will learn to open your energetic blocks, heal the emotional or spiritual holes, or expose your beliefs that are creating blocks in your body. The healing is a method to clear out these unwanted blocks and help gain your flow of energy in the way you were born to flow energetically. Does that make sense?"

"Wow!" I said, "Do I have to *do* anything?"

"No." she reassured me. "It's about relaxing on the massage table and trusting me. I'll be able to talk to you and communicate with you, but I'll also be in a light trance while I'm doing the healing."

We, humans, were built to flow full of energy and naturally

heal our bodies. We are amazing organisms because we possess invisible intuitive healing abilities that occur automatically. Optimizing our health begins by opening our chakras or energy spirals and flowing. The heart creates a powerful electrical field, which leads the rest of the body's physiology. This electrical synchronization is a very powerful healing modality and is always at our command using our intentions and our beliefs. Shamanism is an incredible tool for rejuvenating ourselves after years and years of experiences that may have bruised our souls or even removed parts.

Jade started the energy session by having me lie down and breathe deeply. It was about eleven o'clock on a Friday morning, Good Friday. The room was bright and open. The prospect of welcoming positive energy into my home gave me hope. Jade walked me through a soothing technique, relaxing each muscle from my head to my toes. I was calm. With each breath, I sank more deeply into the table. Then Jade did her standard scanning of my chakras.

The more I sunk into my body; the more acutely aware I became of my bodily sensations and chakra blockages. It took about ten minutes, I focused intently on my breath, believing with each inhale this healing could be filled with surprises and oddities. Jade said my second, fourth, and fifth chakras were blocked. That's the emotion, heart and throat chakras. When my chakras are open, everything feels open and flowing, as it should be. The spaces got muddy and clogged when there are blockages. Sometimes chakras can feel like a cork or knife is in the area. Occasionally physical ailments develop, such as reflux or stomach pain or even gas. I had reflux regularly and often stomach pain. So, I was aware that my second and fifth were blocked, but I didn't detect my heart chakra. I'm less aware of my heart. The second chakra is around the belly button. I could tell when it was full and round. The throat chakra is more natural to detect, it feels hard to breathe when it's blocked. Because of my reflux and indigestion lately, I was looking forward to clearing my chakras with this energy session. Hoping it would help things circulate and flow.

First, she unblocked the second chakra. It's incredible that both Jade and I worked together to visualize the energy and then move it up and out of my body. Jade sent the intentions to move it out of me, support me, along with vibrations of drum beating and rattling. I helped by imagining it leaving or visualizing whatever Jade suggested. It seemed unusual and unlikely that these simple techniques would alleviate anything, but slowly, they did open me to let the painful energy escape and flow. I was amazed, all the sensations going on. Gradually, the energy floated up to my throat. The blocked energy began vibrating and swirling until I could feel it starting to release and float away, little by little it would loosen and then dissipate. I imagined the energy floating up and out my mouth, breathing dark ashes into the air. Each breath brought it higher and moved it out. Eventually, phlegm built up in my throat until I coughed. This cough was a relief, a release of bad energy. My muscles started to move and twitch. I observed the power in my body. I was both vulnerable to be exposed and raw, yet comforted to have Jade supporting me. Floating and arching, my stomach started to feel lighter and emptier, like free space, open, until I was coughing and clearing my throat of the negative energy ball that was forming. Some different type of energy was present, something sticky and strong. I had a "knowing," that it may be an emotion. Jade started having difficulty clearing my chakras completely. She saw an unidentified entity in my throat. An entity is an energy that has needs and intentions. She started focusing on it. Acknowledging pain and blocks was vital to healing. She quickly journeyed or went into a light trance to ask questions to understand the blockages better. She saw a Giraffe and it was choking a bit, or regurgitating. Animals are often symbols used by spirits to convey messages. Great, I thought, I might be regurgitating too!

As we were both working with the energy, it drifted up onto my head, almost clinging to me more than the other energy. Yikes, I was a little worried! It kept slipping higher and higher onto my face. I opened my eyes, looked down and saw my legs. Before every healing, Jade calls in all spirits from the north, the south, the east, the west, the lower world, the upper world, and the middle world. Jade called in all the supportive spirits that can help peel off any unwanted energy. Many spirits were assisting Jade and I, not just her and I. It was Faith and Trust.

I was uncomfortable with this energy stuck on my face, but I also realized there was a lesson for me. Trusting Jade and all the spirits around me, made me feel guarded and supported. Part of me was fighting the strange sensation climbing onto my jawline; somewhat paralyzing, yet part of me knew to be compassionate and curious towards the energy. It felt as if someone wanted me to pay attention to a message. Jade kept asking "Are you alright?"

I was still confident. "Yes!" I answered her. I tried to move it myself by toning, which is like moaning loudly to release energy to get it to release from my throat and face. I thought if I toned thoroughly enough, it would release. Eventually, it was swirling on my mouth, lips, and chin. Jade was trying to help it release. She saw that it needed to give me a message also. I could NOT do it on my own. As she and I both tried to blow on it or suck the thing off me. I told it, that I loved it and that it was helping me. *Thank You.* I thought in my mind. Then I asked nicely for it to leave. To go!

It felt like someone had grabbed my lips and under my chin. My temples were vibrating. Such a strange sensation, yet I still knew I was strong and fine in that sensation. Numbness and tingling were around my lips. I couldn't speak very well, but I kept describing it to Jade. It is surreal to explain something you can't see. It's like seeing its color and shape in your mind's eye and realizing at the same time the importance of this healing and this message.

Finally, the emotion on my face began to speak to me in my mind. It needed to communicate a strong message. Not with a voice, but with a knowing. *Let me come back. I will go, but only if you admit that you need me and let me come back again in the future.* Without being sure, I agreed I needed it in my life and told it that I would allow it to come back, but that I didn't need it right now. *What emotion are you?* I asked.

It answered *I am anger.* It left, very slowly. Later, Jade described it as smoke floating away. I agreed—it sort of slowly lifted off my face in a mist. It had such a grasp on my face; I expected it would slide away or come to a head and burst. But it didn't. It just drifted ever so slowly, into the air. The lightness in my body again left me twitching and shaking; not unlike a release. I freed something very heavy. I was completely lighter and healthier once it was gone, gone entirely. I felt whole!

Now the healing was over, and Jade closed the ritual by smudging with white sage, to clear the air. She lit the white sage and let the smoke cleanse away any negativity in the room or around us.

When we finished, Jade and I were laughing, remembering. I kept imitating how my lips seemed frozen. "That was not normal!" Jade chuckled. "You had freakin' anger on your face!" she laughed.

I was so relieved and grateful; grateful for what seemed like a gift to experience. I kept laughing hard and feeling light and happy. I was like a new body, like a new skin, like new insides, so much lighter and floaty. I was stress-free and almost tickly inside. I was like a kid again, younger, more energetic!

After reflecting on everything, I lay relaxed, listening. Jade read to me what Giraffe means. A giraffe is a bridge, to get from now into the future. It has foresight. It tells me to keep to my future. Don't stop trying. Focus on one idea at a time, rather than all your ideas at once. Even if you don't finish the project, make at least one idea manifest. The vision exists first, then move it into action. The giraffe tells me not to be afraid and to move forward. She also told me to feel my roots. My head is in the clouds, stay connected to Earth. Keep grounding yourself. Let yourself feel anger. Don't just ignore it. Use it, to really feel it, and then let it go. Don't ignore any emotion, or it gets worse and wants to be acknowledged more. Acknowledge the existence of the emotions and then ask it why it's inside you. There are reasons. There is a purpose. Anger taught me to let it in and admit that I need it—and then let anger go. Don't hang on to negative emotions or beliefs! Let it flow through you!

Anger motivates us to actions. It may scare you. It may embarrass you. But it is useful to get you to speak your truth. It is useful to get you to express your deepest needs. The lesson was to realize that anger is not *who* you are; it's only an emotion. Emotions are only passing through to help you, not to harm you. Pain is only passing through to teach you, not to hurt you. The block comes from not releasing the emotion but holding on to it. Ignoring anger makes it occur more often and bigger and stronger. Holding anger at bay prevented me from flowing and healing and functioning at my optimal level.

Reiki

Reiki is a healing technique based on the principle
that the healer can channel energy into the person
by means of touch, to activate the natural
healing processes of the person's body and
restore physical and emotional well-being.

Now that I had released some of my anger, I was freer and more
myself, whole. I was less alone in the universe. There was a broader
meaning to life since anger spoke to me in that healing. I wasn't
responsible for as much as I took responsibility for blaming myself.
Life was a group effort, not just me steering the boat alone. Witnessing
a force much larger and more powerful than me was a relief. I was less
in control and less responsible. Maybe there was some omnipotent,
loving force. It was everywhere. These Shamanic healings offered me
hope; hope that I wasn't numb or negative or weak, hope that I wasn't
useless and lost. I could change. Maybe I was capable of raising my
kids separately from Jackie. I didn't have much faith in my abilities

yet, but I had a newfound faith in Jade's energy work and the answers coming through these healings, answers from an unseen world that was "watching over" me. I never thought about spirituality before. I believed in unseen concepts because I figured it was my choice, to either believe in something larger than me or not. The notion of simply *believing* was better and happier and healthier to me than *not* believing. Spirits or unseen guides were whatever you decided for yourself. Spirit could be as you precisely defined it, not a deity, not some guy on a cloud judging your actions. It felt worth the risk to pursue more answers by asking more questions. With more support, I could be stronger and more confident for my kids. If I could take better care of myself, I would take better care of them. But how?

Secretly, since I was a kid, I wanted superpowers to make me stronger. I wanted to time-travel, read minds, heal the sick, and talk to the dead. I used to ask the universe for signs and sometimes I received them. I really was a dreamer. In high school, I was very superstitious during my volleyball games. I had a routine or touch my jersey or rub my hands together to get luck rolling. I believed in good intentions, magic, miracles, and dreams.

My friend Kerry from work talked of her friend's mother who practiced Reiki. Healing the soccer players in high school, she would run out to the players who got hurt on the field. She laid her hands on the sore muscle of the player and heat and warmth of the energy spread then pain disappeared. "That's so awesome!" I said to Kerry after she told me Reiki stories. "I want to learn to do that!" Fascinated! It was like a superpower to me.

Like a superpower, experiencing healings with Jade was the highlight of my days. She got rid of my reflux, my headaches, opened my heart up, and gave me hope. More sensations were in my body after each healing. Plus, I had a place to address huge questions about my life's purpose, about my kids, about my relationships. I began bringing her those questions and addressing important issues in my life. After about five healings with Jade, I wanted to help other people like she did. I wanted to share the new found method for healing, becoming whole. "How could I get to know energy better like you?" I asked Jade one day at work. "Take a Reiki 1 class!" she advised. "It will introduce you to the feeling of Reiki energy and teach you the basics." So I took a Reiki 1 class. It wasn't like me. I didn't take classes. I never was a joiner. I rarely liked groups, but I did enjoy college and graduate school enough because of playing and coaching volleyball. I gave Reiki a try. Reiki is a Japanese technique of intending energy that is all around you to travel through your body and out your hands to someone else, in order to place their body into a relaxed state for optimum healing. The technique is to become a channel for life force energy using only our bodies and our intention to heal others through touch.

A Reiki advertisement for a class was right in front of me one day, hanging on the wall. Only a mile from my house in the Waxworks building, a textile factory they converted into businesses. The second floor, Spirit Works Healing Arts offered Reiki 1 class in two 4 hour sessions. It began as a small step towards believing in me. Maybe I could heal.

I signed up and came home to tell Jackie I was taking a class. "How much is it?" she asked. "One hundred dollars," I said cautiously. "It will make me money eventually, though" I added, exaggerating the truth. "How many classes is it?" she asked. "Just two classes, two

149

nights," I answered. I waited for more questions, but she just looked down at her photos, she was putting pictures of the kids into a photo album.

Initially, I didn't believe in myself or my ability to give energy. One cold, dark, winter night in December, my first Reiki class in Waxworks included only the teacher, Ingrid, and me, no other students. I was bright red blushing, and my hands were shaking. I didn't know Ingrid, and now I had to put my hands on her in a dim room alone. I didn't like touching people AT ALL!! She lay on the table, and I squirmed. I had no idea how to give Reiki or where to put my hands. My mind was racing. Now the teacher was my first subject. How intimidating!! How can you have a Reiki CLASS with only one participant? It wasn't what I expected. Just put your hands on someone and then what? Still, even feeling insecure and bumbling, the sensations and the good intentions behind sharing the energy intrigued me.

Reiki just flows. You can't do it wrong. It's about relaxing into it and not stressing about the RIGHT anything. Step aside so that the energy can flow, no judgment. I did the wrong thing when I began, I judged, I was worried I'd do it wrong. Then one day in class, I honestly felt the energy! For real!! It started as a tingle, and then grew into a heated sensation flowing down my arms and into my hands. Cold hands turned hot with my intention to heal behind it. I was surprised how much I sensed. When I questioned it, it disappeared. When I feared it, it disappeared. I practiced the techniques Ingrid said to help the Reiki flow easier and faster because, in the first class, I didn't always believe it, so I didn't always do it. The methods that improved the flow of Reiki were clearing the mind, blanking out your thoughts, deeply relaxing, breathing, and trusting Reiki would come. And then it did!!! It really did flow like a faucet, warm and tangible.

We all have energy inside, but most of us don't believe in ourselves. We have that inner critic or ego telling us we aren't worthy and we don't have the ability to heal, yet we do. I wondered why we get so scared. Drive 80 miles an hour in a car; you feel safe? But touching someone? Too risky? I'm curious why we would rather have needles stuck in our skin, or have some clinical procedure, rather than touch each other. Touch is vulnerable, more vulnerable than most people can handle. But touching was always awkward at first. I never liked people touching me, especially strangers. I started out skeptical and not trusting others, or my ability to have a flow of energy. Witnessing many different students, one by one change from nervousness to wide-eyed expressions of experiencing the sensations of Reiki was convincing. One day in Reiki class, it occurred to me. What if healing and love and life force energy were surrounding us like air, but we didn't believe in it? What if we merely kept ourselves separate from it, yet it was right there? Imagine if you ignored it or cut yourself off from it, rather than invite it in or use it to navigate life. What if you could tap into it at any time during our lives? What if we could be joyous, happy, and free most of the time? I'd rather believe. Why not trust, rather than risk missing all that possibility, all that potential? It's a choice to use it or not use it. It's a gift we can accept or ignore. I accept. We all have life force energy at our fingertips for free. All of us!!

Ingrid stood at the head of a massage table and put her hands on someone's head. I stood two tables down from the three tables set up in the class, my hands on someone else's arms. Making eye contact with her and my other Reiki friends, knowing our intentions were to heal, I was basking in the good energy filling the room. It was invigorating and powerful. I enjoyed holding space with all types of people in those classes and being silent at the same time. Reiki opened a new way to let love into my life, to open to others, in silence, sending wishes. During Reiki, I let go of the questioning and the fear, and it made space in my heart for something better. An energy I had never expected began to expand within me.

Then I took Reiki 2 class, and I was further hooked on the medium. Reiki 2 teaches the student how to send and intend healing energy into the past, the future and into any situation you choose. Absentee Reiki means you aren't touching, only intending the energy into another person; they can be across the country. Sending energy was meditative. It was like prayer. It helped me soothe what was coming into my life as well as the past that seemed impossible to forget. Sending Reiki as I went to interviews helped. Sending Reiki prior to public presentations helped me be less nervous. Sending Reiki was methodical and empowering, calming and peaceful.

I was so impressed with Reiki and the positive influences it had on my health and confidence; I was motivated to become a Reiki Master Teacher. After two years of studying and co-teaching several Reiki 1 and two classes and many hours of individual healing sessions, I earned my certification as a Reiki Master Teacher. A lot happened during those two years of learning and sharing Reiki. One day during that time, I was picking up my kids after gymnastics. On the YMCA playground, a bunch of the kids were playing, and one of the older girls smashed her elbow on a metal bar, and her hand had seized in a clinched position, almost frozen that way. She was crying a little, and I immediately grabbed her elbow and gave her Reiki. As I did, I asked her mom if it was OK I give her Reiki, and she agreed. The other mothers were getting frantic and discussing sending her to the doctor and telling her to get some ice. I stayed confident with her and looked her in the face. I caught a glimpse of my kids watching me give Reiki to our friend. The Reiki flowed fast and healed her. Her hand relaxed and the moment was over. She was back to normal in about 3 minutes. Healed, I let go of all judgments.

Another amazing new tool I acquired from Reiki was quieting my mind and reframing my thoughts from scarcity to abundance. In class, Ingrid set up chairs in a circle facing outward as she walked around us and guided us through a meditation. I sat comfortably, feet flat on the ground, notebook at my side. "Close your eyes, notice your breathing, imagine long roots going into the ground, feel them wrap around your ankles, reaching down through the dirt, deep into the earth." Imagining came easy to me, but I noticed the part of my mind that criticized and judged everything began to quiet down over more and more meditations in Reiki class. Its tone softened. Its frequency decreased. The most useful way of channeling Reiki is thinking of nothing, picturing a cloud, staying clear of worry. As Ingrid led the class, she suggested something I had not thought of ever before, in all my study of Psychology. "We all try to heal our past mistakes and analyze flaws already established and relive memories to heal." She suggested we invest in the future. Imagine our best outcomes. How about trusting in a bright future with abundance of everything, rather than lack or worry? What would life look like if we believed we had everything we need from now on? It caused me to let go of worry so that I could hang onto abundance. Suddenly I was seeing myself standing in mountain pose, rather than hanging by a wire looking down. I was acknowledging that my thoughts held me in a place that may not be true at all, acknowledging that my thoughts were hindering my growth, preventing my happiness.

Reiki teaches five basic principles to attain happiness; 1) Just for today, I will let go of anger. 2) Just for today, I will let go of worry. 3) Just for today, I will be grateful. 4) Just for today, I will do my work honestly. 5) Just for today, I will be kind to every living thing, including myself. 'Just for today,' keeps you focused on the present. Letting go of anger and worry I had practiced with Jade in my healings. These simple principles helped guide me to take small steps towards happiness, stable reminders, similar to several other spiritual guideposts. Reiki began as a mystery to me. The concept of healing and energy amazed me. Shamanism stirred my energy intensely; it made me want to heal the way Jade did. Reiki was more practical for my learning. It suited me. The energy was subtle, calming, and relaxing. The tingly vibration moved like electric as my hands were placed on people, but often, I doubted all of it, particularly myself. After a lot of practice, it occurred to me again, when I cleared out my thoughts, the flow of energy came through me more, like a water faucet. I had to trust it was there, or nothing happened. Letting go of worry, Reiki flowed full force. Any negativity or self-doubts prevented the natural flow or at least slowed it down.

Humans have incredible powers, but most of us don't believe it. And not believing in our abilities is enough resistance to block the opportunity of it. The energy was real, more heat and more tingling occurring in my hands and fingers. A constant tingling wrapped around my upper back and arms. The more I believed and trusted my own strengths, the more sensations I experienced. I could channel energy!! When I feel that sensation of tingling, even now, I know its energy. Reiki taught me to allow the life force energy into my body from below and above, imagining it flowing through my head and my feet to my arms. The energy was not coming *from* my body; it was coming *through* my body, like a hollow tree trunk. The difference was huge. Every class, I gained more Faith in my own ability to channel energy or heal, and in the many things I couldn't see with my eyes.

I visited my parents in Pennsylvania one day and was standing in my former bedroom. There on the shelf, a book caught my attention. It read, "Tai Chi classics" by Waysun Liao. The book was my mom's. She was taking Tai Chi classes and wanted to learn more about Tai Chi movement. Ironically, the book was more about transferring power or chi, meaning energy in China, through your body. In the book, there were drawings of how energy or power is pulled from the ground up the legs and into the waist and then moved through the breath and out the hands. This was everything I was learning in Reiki classes. But they were using as a martial art to attack and defend. I was amazed at how many centuries these studies were taught in China. I skimmed through the book drawings, and it said, "chi is greatly improved with much meditation and imagination." There were diagrams of the feet and the breath almost exactly as we learned in Reiki. Knowing I had a vivid imagination, I committed to daily meditation to improve my energy and power.

In my Reiki classes, I had first-hand observations of so many people feeling similar sensations when giving and receiving Reiki. I was required to perform more than 100 hours of Reiki through classes and healing sessions with friends and volunteers. All the experiences were positive and enlightening. Two of the highlights of those experiences were when John Dempsey Hospital allowed me to give a public presentation, educating nurses about the strength and benefits of Reiki. Looking out at the crowd from the stage, Jade and Gloria listened intently to my talk. My slides showed how we all vibrate and are connected to one another. I taught the nursing students that Reiki energy is positively helpful and can't cause any side effects, like medications. There is nothing harsh or invasive. There are no risks, yet it is powerful. I set up a Reiki table before and after the talk so nurses could experience Reiki first hand. They laid down and received 10 minutes of Reiki to feel the energy. Many of them were open and kind and thanked me for the relaxing sensations.

As she passed by my table, one of the nurses told me she couldn't receive Reiki because it was blasphemy to her. For her, anything that was not Christian or created from Jesus Christ was from Satan, so she couldn't understand why I would ever give Reiki if it were from Satan. I understood her fear and thanked her for her honesty. Fear-based thoughts like that one were proof to me that religions are created from the ego mind, not the spirit, not the heart. How did Jesus heal with his hands? Wasn't Jesus human? As a human, I believe I'm created by something good, not evil. All people are blessed with good inside and healing is our birthright.

Another experience was meeting regularly with my own volunteers as I trained to learn Reiki in personal sessions. My friend Greta's husband, Steven was conservative and skeptical, but he had bad arthritis in his right hand, around his thumb and also in his lower back. He loved golfing, so he agreed to do Reiki every other week with me. In one enlightening session, I was giving Reiki, and I saw clouds and the sky lowered into reds and orange. He usually fell asleep during the session and snored, but not this time. I set my two hands on his sore arthritic thumb, and his arm slowly twitched as I kept my hands there for about 10 minutes, which seemed like a very long time. My hands grew very, very hot on his meaty thumb. As I moved to put my hands on his head, I could feel tingling through my entire body. More visions of sky passed through my mind. When I finished, Steven swung his legs around to sit up and said, "Oh my God. I feel no pain at all! I haven't felt this good in so long!" He kept opening and closing his sore hand and frowning down at his palm. He was groggy, but rubbed his eyes and said, "I saw these visions of clouds of red and orange. I saw tons of visions!" he said. "That was something!" Usually, Steven didn't describe too much detail to his experience, but he admitted he saw visions and his pain was gone. After he slowly left my table, he usually went upstairs to go straight to sleep. We had many sessions together, but he exemplified how Reiki relieves pain from arthritis. It was gratifying to help Steven.

For me, Reiki helped me calm myself in my relationship with Jackie, handle the stress of raising my kids, deal better with my own life changes, stay focused on my personal goals, and overall lowered my stress levels while my living situation and financial situations were highly unpredictable. I gave Reiki to myself and my kids as a supportive treatment. Reiki practitioners also gave me Reiki at the Reiki Share to help me rejuvenate weekly.

As my comfort with Reiki grew, so did my faith. Maria got a really bad fever once, and I gave her Reiki during the whole illness. I had both hands on her back as she laid on the couch sleeping. I kneeled at her side. I took her temperature before and after Reiki and the fever considerably dropped after receiving Reiki. For Noah, when I put him to sleep at night, I gave him Reiki. He talked and talked and talked, but when I put my hands on him, and he instantly fell asleep. It became magic. Another time, Maria had a stomach bug and putting my hands on her low back and stomach calmed the pain. She kept asking me to put my warm hands on her. Just the tool and the intention helped decrease our anxiety. Ma had Reiki; it could help.

Jackie walked in the room when I was giving Reiki to Maria. She offered Ibuprofen. Being a nurse, she went quickly to Ibuprofen; it was her cure-all. Prior to me taking Reiki, she and Anya gave care using herbals and tinctures. Jackie withheld her opinion when it came to taking Reiki classes. She felt energy work was her thing, not mine. It was early on in our relationship when she was studying Nursing at UMass she took holistic nursing classes and wanted to incorporate more energy and natural therapy to help patients, but not since the kids came. Once I started my own discovery of energy, she never discussed it much. Yet, she never discouraged me from giving Reiki.

At times, I still got scared. I still felt doubts. I still got stressed, but when I did, I called on the energy as a friend or a guide. The point is to accept scared, accept doubts, acknowledge them and then let them go. Sometimes I simply burned white sage to feel better. Other times I beat on my drum to change the energy in the room or in my body. I also called on Reiki and my fellow Reiki practitioners for a sense of being loved and supported. Discussing things with them helped me. To me, Reiki became my personal tool for better self-care, better flow. When I took good care of myself, then it made me a better person, a better Ma. My shine came back. I was less anxious, calmer, more loving, and I became more confident.

Forgiveness

Forgiveness is the act of
ending a feeling of anger or resentment toward
someone for an offense, flaw, or mistake.

The day before my forty-second birthday, I woke to a raging headache and abdominal pain. Rarely do I ever get headaches. My vision was blurry, my heart sad. My evil supervisor had decided the day before that I should not be allowed to continue to telecommute twice a week, and that I should go to work instead. "Sorry Alison, but several employees have been complaining that you telecommute. I know you've been doing it for 13 years, but Human Resources told us that you are forbidden to do it anymore," he said with a smirk. Over the ten years I worked with my supervisor, he stole data, yelled and lied to co-workers, and manipulated young medical students. He was a troubled soul. He used to say my job was the same as working at Staples, shuffling forms. He was a very insecure power monger. I didn't want to work with this guy any longer. A few days after, I elected to resign half my hours and lose half my salary so that I could be with my kids twice a week instead. It was a way out of my push-pull days of telecommuting. Rather than drive 65 miles for five days of the week, I concluded that my kids were more important than money. It was a blessing not to have to be split between work and kids anymore. Initially, I was angry with my department heads' for manipulating me, but deep down, I was relieved that I was finally going to stop telecommuting.

Jade was there at work when they took my telecommuting away. I went into her cubicle and told her about the whole incident. The two bumbling idiots who wanted to destroy any sign of friendship or comradery in our department. Jade advised thinking longer about resigning before acting on it, but I had already made up my mind. I'm not leaving my kids five days a week. "There's no amount of money," I said indignantly. "I'm not putting more time into this place when they don't even care about me. I'd rather dedicate my time to loving my kids! I'll live on the streets happy rather than sell my soul to this place!" I strode to my cubicle pissed off. I began drafting a letter that same day at my desk. "I'm sorry I have to resign to 50% of my time because Human Resources will no longer allow me to telecommute." My common sense convinced me to wait a few days to deliver the letter. In retrospect, I never received anything in writing from Human Resources or any complaints, so it may have simply been a lie from my department heads to get me to resign halftime. I'll never know. In the end, it improved my life. I wouldn't change a thing.

At the time, I didn't even discuss it with Jackie. I was dividing into my own person. My decision was for my family, but I was the one deciding. I was the one making a decision. Clear-headed and confidently, that was the right thing to do, be with my kids.

The day after, my head was killing me! It must be from the work change. I intuited a message telling me to "trust and reach out" for help. So I called Jade by that afternoon because the pain was getting worse between my eyes. Headaches were rare. Ibuprofen hadn't touched it at all. And something told me this headache was more energy and negativity than a physical ailment. I had already done three healing sessions with Jade at her home, but this would be my first time having energy work done over the phone. To be precise, I was stretched out on my couch, with my kids nearby as always. I didn't think I was sick or coming down with anything. It was difficult for me to ask for help, but I was trying to reach out more than I used to. It was 4:30 pm and the kids were watching TV on the one couch while I lay comfortably on the smaller couch in the living room. I figured it would only be a few minutes on the phone with Jade, me relaxing, her rattling and then she could send me some healing love and light. Thank you very much. But what happened was so much more personal and intimate and life-changing.

"Hello!" she greeted me. "I'm going to begin by scanning your body for blockages in your chakras and other general assessment of issues you might be experiencing." My hands were sweaty, my pulse twitching in my ears. All I had to do was breathe and surrender, yet it was all so focused; as if she was reading my mind and also reading my body. Jade had no idea what issue to work on in this session. I told her that I had a headache with lots of pressure. Like plugging in, Jade gathered more reasons through her Shamanic methods why I had a headache. Several minutes passed that Jade said nothing, maybe six minutes. The silence felt like forever. What was she DOING? I stared at the ceiling, listening to my breathing through the receiver.

She came back on the line and told me, "You have three blocks; in your heart chakra (4th), your throat chakra (5th) and your third eye or forehead chakra (6th)." I agreed. Then she said, "Do you have any feelings of regret or unresolved issues?"

"No," I bleated. I drew a blank. "No idea—nothing I can think of," I said, absently.

Obviously, I was clouded by something big. Why didn't I admit my rage at Jackie? My judgment was off on a lot of things regarding Jackie. But the dance we had was home to me, the push-pull, the love-hate. She was home. Was I ready to step away from home? No, it was familiar and safe. It was usual to rail against her and blame her and be angry at her. All that prevented me from the honest, raw truth of our relationship. Fear kept me dependent on Jackie for many facets of my life. Yes, I certainly was afraid of her. But, in another part of my brain, I believed Jackie was a good person, my friend. She was my wife. With her as my scapegoat, I could keep avoiding responsibility for my own fears and lack of actions. Blinders on tight, I truly didn't see any pending forgiveness necessary to move forward in my life.

Jade explained further, "I'm being told by the Spirits that you aren't distressed by work or the telecommuting loss, but by your personal life. You cannot see or focus on your goals clearly because you are blocked by unresolved anger towards something, or someone. You need to forgive someone. You're clouded with negative emotions." I thought of ex-girlfriends, like Samantha or Mindy, but nothing really clicked until Jade kept saying, "Forgiveness is very healing."

Then, like a blinding light, I finally realized that I had not forgiven Jackie for reducing Noah's womb siblings from 3 babies to 1. I explained to Jade that we had tried to get pregnant for years and finally had gotten pregnant through artificial insemination and fertility drugs, but it was triplets. "We had three boys growing inside Jackie," I told her, "but Jackie elected for a fetal reduction three and a half years ago, during Noah's pregnancy. Aborting two babies on purpose felt so wrong in my heart—like destroying a true gift from the universe. I could never elect to reduce after such extents to get pregnant. It felt too controlling, too much in the hands of science and not enough in faith. I've been so angry at her. I'm still holding on to the regret and anger of reducing."

Even though I now knew I was still angry with Jackie, I wondered what that had to do with today's headache. But when I told Jade I was still angry and holding it in my body, she revealed, "I got chills when you talked about the reduction of the babies. Yes indeed—that is your emotional block!"

Straightaway, Jade swung into the next phase of healing. "OK, you're going to imagine your heart, red and full." She guided me. "You're going to see your heart, and it's a rosebud. Imagine it opening, see it opening and blossoming into a full flower. See the beautiful, red flower and all its satin petals. Then see droplets of water on the petals of the flower. See the drops of water clearly on the soft, velvety petals. Now imagine a tunnel in the water droplet, and look down the tunnel. Imagine that you see Jackie coming through the tunnel. Send Jackie blessings and love and say to her what you need, in order to forgive her. Take some time right now, and say to her what you need to open your heart and forgive her. There's no need to hold on to the regret or anger towards her. Say what you need to forgive Jackie."

That's when it was my turn to focus. I breathed deeply. A resistance to the emotion came first. Then, there was a building tension rising in my chest. I reached toward the tender feeling, rather than looking away or ignoring it. I searched for a sentence to express myself. It bubbled up slowly, nauseous yet emotional.

I wanted a chance to raise those boys! I wanted a chance! I yelled at Jackie in my mind. As I admitted the words silently, every cell in my body swelled, expanded, and opened, including my heart. The tears in my eyes and face and the swollen lumpy cry got stuck in my throat. I arched my back off the couch a bit and almost cried out, tightening in sadness, pain, burning in my chest. It was one of the most emotional moments of my entire life.

Afterward, Jade's voice came so softly on the line, and she said, "I felt you crying and felt my heart open." Jade told me to send Jackie more blessings and love and forgiveness. She rescanned my chakras and confirmed that my heart had indeed opened.

"Now," she said, "it's time to open your throat chakra. I want you to picture the shape and color of your blockage." I said it was a triangle and I couldn't think of a color. She said to see the shape and color in my mind's eye and then "blow it into the balloon." She said, "to fill the balloon up with the blockage in your throat."

I focused on my throat. I vividly saw the color leave in bits, dusty bits filled the balloon, and then I imagined it floating out the window. Jade again rescanned and confirmed. I had cleared it by imagining those dusty bits floating away. In my throat, muscles were cleaner and more relaxed. I tried to do the same with my head blockage, but it didn't leave. It was stuck to me. My head felt stickier and heavier. Then she said the third eye needed her help. She said it was not moving and I needed to help her get it out. And then she asked a powerful question: "Are you ready to let it go? Because…I'm going to get it out."

I confirmed confidently, "Yes, I'm ready to let it go."

This was where all my pain had been parked all day; on the back of my skull and in my right eyebrow, it had sat there, throbbing. Pain swirled at the center of my skull and then trickled toward the front.

Jade set the phone down, and I heard nothing, but sensed more swirling within and then I visualized an upside-down tornado pulling out of my forehead as I heard her inhale it with a breath. The pain was considerably less. It was incredibly instant! Even in the midst of tears and my sinuses swollen from crying so hard, I could feel the pain subside, and my head was so much lighter and more open. Then I detected more energy in my right eye, some pain. Jade came on the phone again, "I have to extract again to remove all of it."

I agreed because of the remaining pain in my head. For the second time, she set the phone down; the last tornado exited my head like a horn breaking off and floating away. Jade coughed the negative energy into a bowl of salt water.

As Jade coughed, so did Noah. He had been next to me on the couch, unaware of why he coughed. He coughed for his brothers, he coughed for me, and he coughed for Jackie. The negative energy was out, and I was so relieved!

Jade offered, "I'm crying too, and I felt your sadness around the boys' loss." She could sense I opened my third eye. She advised,

"Open the window and smudge yourself and the house with white sage."

My pain was gone. Together we let it go. We released it. I forgave Jackie.

Later, my head had some tiny inklings of pain, but it left, bit by bit. I had fallen asleep an hour later and stayed asleep for 3 hours. Around 10 pm, I woke up to tell Jackie about my experience. "Can I tell you about today?" I asked. Her eyes looked worried as I began speaking to her. "Apparently I needed to forgive you still, after the reduction." I began to divulge.

"You've been angry at me for many years," she said. "You don't realize how mean you are to me, or how rude you talk to me," she began to cry.

I ignored her. *Say what you need to tell her*. I went on. "I forgive you for everything. Jade did a healing on me over the phone. She had me envision you coming out of a rose. It was meditative and therapeutic! I was moved and felt so much relief after she sucked the energy away," I spoke quickly and excitedly about the healing.

She offered very little in response—just asked me, "Is that it?"

"Yeah," I sighed. Part of me wanted her to be excited about my healings. Part of me wanted her to say something. The sensations and emotions after my healings were so incredibly energizing and uplifting and full of contentment and satisfaction. I wanted to tell EVERYONE! But forgiveness can be a judgment. Forgiveness is much more for the person doing the forgiving, not the person being forgiven. It was for me. The healing was only for me. Still, I ached to share these experiences with everyone and anyone.

These healings were usually monthly, but they helped me tremendously. It was inside work, inner growth. I was dropping my negative judgments and learned to accept the negative. "You suck" changed to "You deserve to be happy." Eeyore was in my head before. "This won't work. Don't get used to it" changed to "Everything can work! If you change now, you can make it better again also! Get used to win-win!" Smiling was easier, more natural. My body felt lighter, stronger. In Reiki classes, people told stories of walking again after being crippled. We discovered that most of the first Reiki practitioners were teachers because they could not recover their health using conventional medicine and tried Reiki, where they healed from cancer and other major illnesses.

Like a monthly treatment, I visited Jade to receive a healing and talk with her. She was a good friend as well as an excellent healer in Shamanism. Her kind and gentle ways made it easy to work with her. I was moved by her dedication and her willingness to help with nothing in return. Mostly she appreciated my experiences and how it helps us both grow as people. She honestly liked helping people. She genuinely wanted what was best for me, so did I. We had been friends and colleagues for more than 15 years. Now guided by the unseen spirit world, these healings gave me such incredible support. More than I've ever known in my life, more than therapy, simple support by believing in me and offering energy. The antidote for anxiety was Love energy. It was exactly what I needed to feel better about myself and raise my kids better.

Magic Green Fairy

A Fairy is a small imaginary being of
human form that has magical powers,
especially a female one.

Around my twelfth healing with Jade, I drove south to Connecticut on
a Sunday. I pulled into her driveway crying about Jackie. Before I left
my house, we argued about my resentfulness towards her. "Why can't
you just thank me?" she said. "Why aren't you grateful that I support
you in these healings?" I was surprised. I was caught off guard. I took
inventory of my feelings. I didn't feel ungrateful. Was I? On my way
to Jade's, I left Jackie a voicemail telling her I was grateful to her for
letting me go for a healing.

When we settled in her sacred room, Jade began, "What are
your goals for this healing session?"

I had been feeling fat and loathing myself for not being
athletic anymore, not motivated to run or exercise. Triggered by my
clothing, I always wore the same size since I was sixteen. I was held to
higher standard. My grandmother, my mother, even my sister
dedicated much of their lives to their bodies, to staying young, to

being fit. We were willful and controlled. Comments on other women's bodies like, "Can you believe she looks like that now? She really let herself go!" To cope, they all exercised like crazy! I'd rather play and relax, meditate, and not stress about diet or exercise. I hated my weight gain, still holding expectations of my twenties. Up and down with my exercise habits, I wanted to know why it was getting harder to lose weight or exercise. Those physical activities were growing more and more insignificant in my daily routine, and self-loathing crept into my self-talk. I didn't want my self-loathing for myself or my kids. "Well, I want to work on my body image issues, but I also feel like I should address another topic. A topic that had me crying on my way here. Why don't I feel grateful to Jackie for allowing me this time to do energy work?" I whined. "Why do I still feel anger towards Jackie instead of gratefulness?" I asked.

Muscle testing or kinesiology is a technique used to find answers without relying on our egos or our 'me-minds.' Usually, Jade uses this technique to lead us through the plan and to find answers to my questions about life. I held out my left arm straight, and Jade asked questions "Is it most useful for Alison to focus on her body image issues today?" Then she pushed on my arm for an answer. If my arm weakens or drops low as she pushed, then that meant "no." But if I stayed strong and solid with resistance to her pushing, then that's "yes." The trick was for me to be consistent with my arm tension and Jade's pushing should be consistent with the amount of pressure. Jade was trained thoroughly on muscle testing. The whole idea was to allow your body to answer the questions, rather than your ego. It is believed and proven with research that our body's muscles will weaken at false statements and strengthen at true statements.

With this in mind, using muscle testing, Jade cleared away my other goals and narrowed down my issue to "remove the obstacles that prevent me from expressing gratefulness to Jackie." The obstacle was a future obstacle, not present or past. Next, I had to ask myself in my mind, by meditating, what the obstacles were to me. Sitting in a lounge chair opposite Jade, she asked me to sink inside the feeling. My chest felt tight and heavy. There was tension in my throat, my teeth. Tears were coming immediately, which meant my thoughts were on track towards a tender issue. I blurted, "I'm afraid I might physically hurt Jackie if I don't speak up soon." Recently, we had a few ferociously fierce fights, once I actually threatened to throw a chair at her. The vision of that scene flashed quickly through my mind. I had stood up to her, but by threatening her physically. I had picked up a child's chair and faked throwing it at her, but I was furious. "I don't want to hurt her," I said. Jackie provoked it. There was enough anger inside of me to hurt her. "I don't want to be overpowering or violent ever." That's not who I am. I choose not to be angry or violent. I was ashamed of my temper.

Jade confirmed through muscle testing, "yes" this was the focus of today's session. To avoid more anger, I had to do something new, a new action was required. Again we muscle tested until we came up with some stories or the narrative of what I should do. "Let's sink into the feeling again," Jade coached. "What does it look like to avoid anger?" Tears again came, the sound of leather squeaking under me as I shifted and cried more in the lounge chair. Nothing was coming. I needed Jackie "get better," or to act differently. I was angry about our last fight about money. "I didn't want someone to have any control over my money......never to make me feel bad about money again!" Jackie told me I couldn't make decisions about where to spend our money. "Why do we always have to do what you want to do with our money because of your anxiety?" she yelled. "Why did we get new windows and a furnace, instead of the pergola that I wanted?" I don't like feeling vulnerable or attached to a person who can be so rude and selfish. I guarded myself against her. She guarded herself against me also. I wanted to break free from Jackie. She was the obstacle.

I said out loud, "Jackie is preventing me from my path." With each of my thoughts and feelings, I described to Jade what I was feeling and envisioning. She muscle tested on herself to confirm my narrative. She validated and said "yes" or "that's right." I was angry at Jackie for being an obstacle on my path of life. She was preventing me from being myself and thriving. I was trying to be Authentic, but I was not supported.

Through more muscle testing, Jade asked if I could help myself remove or release the negative energy. She pushed on my arm, "Yes, with an intervention, an extraction. As I lay on the massage table, I was tight, tighter than I had ever felt in my life. Jade went to get something for a few minutes, and I became acutely aware of how my stony blocked energy. Not relaxed. *Okay, my head, let go, shoulders, let go.* Down the body, I tried to exhale the stress. Nothing was budging or relaxing. Something was *on* me. Incredible anger sat on my chest.

The healing process began, the minute the rattle sounded, my energy levitated and my body felt heavy, like my spirit separated, then floated up, while my bodily form remained anchored down. Tingling began in the center of my back and wrapped around my shoulders and the tops of my arms. The tingling started to flood around the back of my thighs and my calves. The tingling was spirit, no doubt. I could feel energy fill in around me like water as if my body were being set down into water.

Jade then placed crystals on my chakras. I smelled the tobacco she smoked through a small wooden pipe and a type of alcohol for cleansing to clear negative energy called Florida water. The sweet scents of tobacco and Florida water opened me and grounded me. She had a Shamanic altar or table with many different aids for healings, such as crystals and feathers and a hand drum and a bowl of salt water. All necessary components of a Shamanic healer, always within her reach during a healing. I kept getting intense messages. I started asking for spirit to keep coming in, inside my mind. A voice or thought told me, *The only way to get rid of the energy is to go up and out through the seventh chakra*—the top of my head.

I heard Jade do the first extraction. She had sucked air and energy through her fist in the shape of a circle on my stomach. She made a loud sound with her mouth, like sucking through a straw. The feeling got more intense, and there was a grip around my heart. I envisioned something wrapped around my heart like ribbons; then I saw it in my imagination. The tightness around my left clavicle and the back of my neck were blazing hot and tight and felt like a screw being turned into my bone. Jade tried to suck the energy out with her mouth again, and nothing happened. The energy moved faster and faster.

She started for the drum and began to beat on the hand drum loud at my chest! Relief came with the vibration of the drum. I heard a voice in my head tell me to "vibrate higher" and "think loving thoughts" as the drum moved over my heart. I trusted it. I followed it. I followed what Jade did, in the dark, my eyes closed. We worked together intuitively. I became more determined. Powerful. Stronger than life. Many spirits were helping us.

After the drumming, I could sense things were moving more and lifting off. I began to pray for spirit to take the bad energy and to protect Jade. She had sucked it out and was coughing and gagging into the salt water bowl. I prayed to allow Jade to take it but not to stick to her. Praying to myself, *Please keep us both safe and loved.* At some point, I was nauseous and wished for more tobacco, and just then, Jade blew it over me.

Grounding feels like a floor. I was incredibly grounded by the tobacco scent. It was helpful, earthy, calming, and the nausea dissipated. After more than four tries, Jade asked if it was gone and I told her I could feel just a remnant of tightness—the grip of some kind of bad energy, maybe anger—hiding behind my left clavicle.

Jade used more Florida water and grabbed my left clavicle between her thumb and pointer finger, without my telling her to grab there. She was guided to it. The pressure released with the Florida water. I was tremendously lighter. It was her last extraction ever. I never needed another again.

In the end, slowing down, Jade's hands held on my calves. Often I couldn't tell where she was in the room; the energy was so engulfing, the relaxation so deep. She gave energy to my feet and then my head. I cried a bit more at the images of me and my kids holding hands and hugging flashed through my mind. I spent the rest of the session crying. She propped me up to put her hands on my back and chest at the same time to send love to my heart.

173

Suddenly, I saw a vision of myself about ten years old. I stood there, staring at myself. I sent "young me" blessings. *You are safe. Your life is amazing. You are a good person.* A deep voice in my head resonated loudly; *You are whole. You are whole.* There was such pure deep unconditional love.

To finish, as I lay there, Jade took out her pendulum to confirm whether my chakras were open. She said I was more open than she had ever felt me to be. There was nothing but spirit in my body now—no pain, no bad energy, nothing stopping me from being fully me. It felt like I could float away.

I sat up, and we compared stories during the healing. We had been getting the same messages, and I was amazed that all of our visions were so strikingly similar. I laughed and asked her, "Did you see the energy go behind my clavicle?"

"Yeah!" She smiled. Jade had seen not only the energy hiding in my clavicle but also the young me.

I sat on her massage table and gulped down two glasses of water. Whew! We finished with a bit more muscle testing to give me homework and follow-up. I had to prevent the intervention from fading away and becoming blocked again. By telling Jackie something had to change: either she would get help, or I would get help with her, whether by attending counseling, going to therapy, or doing something different. I had to tell her she needed to let me go if she didn't do something different to make herself healthier. That was my homework. I was on a mission. Could I stand up to her?

I got home and sat on the patio. Then I thought about filling the hummingbird feeder . . . And then I saw one. She flitted in like a magic green fairy and drank three times. Then she flew off.

That night, Jackie and I talked about issues between us, which was rare and unusual. I told her about my healing, but she didn't believe in the spirit world much. She did, however, believe in energy. We discussed our arguments and tried to find common ground, but she didn't understand where I was coming from. "I feel like you never compromise with me," I said. "I try to tell you my feelings or what I need, and then you say how you feel. Neither of us listens." I said.

"But you're so angry with me." She teared up.

The common problem between us was she needed me to hear her, and I needed her to listen to me, but neither of us was willing to give empathy to the other. I tried to be the one to make peace more often, but usually, it just meant I got more angry and resentful. So my technique of trying to be the "bigger" or "more mature" partner in the relationship wasn't working.

I took a deep breath. My hands were steady. Then I said the words, "Either I need you to change, or I'm leaving. I can't keep doing this. What we're doing isn't working for either of us."

"I'm sorry," she said immediately. "I love you. I'm trying so hard to change for you, but it feels like I can't ever please you. You're so angry with me about reducing the boys."

I ignored her comment and responded with, "But I can't keep going like this. I can't keep arguing." She voted to try to change by starting an antidepressant and going to more couples' therapy. *Oh, crap*, I thought. *I don't want to do any of that. I wanted to end this!* Despite my heartfelt desires, I consented to her meds and therapy as a trial fix.

Unfortunately, she started the antidepressant the week we were leaving for vacation to Maine. We always went to Maine for two weeks during the summer, but it was much more packing with a dog and two kids. Instead of helping me get organized to leave that week, Jackie just lay on the couch, shaking. "I can't move!" she hollered. "I have a headache, and my legs are twitching." Her head was spinning. Her appetite was gone. Her sleep was disturbed. She couldn't keep taking that horrible drug. She lay there on the couch spasming while I packed everything up.

The kids were running around the house and trying to help, but they were freaking out that Mama was flat out on the couch. "Ma?" Maria asked me, "Can Mama make it to the beach?"

"Yes, Maria, she'll be fine," I said, although I doubted it, seeing her writhing around in pain. I told all of them that I'd take care of everything, and we headed off to Maine in a messy pile. I could pack, but it wasn't easy to do alone. Maybe she was reacting to the drug. Maybe it was a side effect. Or perhaps she didn't ever want to take antidepressants. To comply with me, she took them for one month. While we were on vacation, I told her to stop. "Please don't take the medication if they make you feel that horrible," I told her. "Are you sure?" she asked. "Yes, you can't feel that bad again," I said. Sometimes we do things we don't want to do; then our bodies tell us to stop. And sometimes we do whatever it takes to survive.

While we were in Maine, she seemed better, and I was worse. Even on vacation, I was uptight and resentful. Jackie packed our days with activities I didn't want to do. I escaped in the morning with Sienna, my dog, on the beach for walks. I enjoyed playing with my kids on the beach and in the ocean. But one afternoon, I ended up defending myself to Jackie again, when she suddenly threatened me. She was yelling and pointing in my face. I was tired and defensive. "If you don't stop being so grumpy and miserable to us this summer, then you better get the hell out of the house by this Fall!" she threatened me. *This Fall, This Fall, This Fall*, echoed in my mind. Every cell in my body woke up! I heard another way out of my marriage. I wanted out. I heard the threat of being thrown out, and I wanted to make it come true. Every fiber of my being longed to leave her; that seemed bad, yet I was relieved. I said nothing.

My dreams at this time were vivid and supportive. In one dream, a black panther called me outside the door of my house, walking beside each window on the outside, as I walked by windows on the inside. We watched each other. The panther had a calm power to it. It was part of me. It casually coaxed me. It sat down at the front door, looking in casually like a cat does. I was trying to heal, to change. When I woke up, I looked up the meaning of "Panther totem" online. Often our dreams have symbolism or meaning to help us understand our current situation. Panther symbolizes our power, strength, courage, and valor. Panther teaches us to improve our understanding of our dark side and to eliminate fears. Similar to many of my past lessons, the panther was telling me to use my anger and strength to get out of the house. It was literally at my door waiting outside, almost daring me to leave. The dream alluded to my power being outside of my present home life.

During the next few weeks, we fought again regularly. I was tired of fighting about money and control and chores. I was so sick of trying to get Jackie to *see* me, to believe and trust me! To try to convince her everything would be OK. But she never took comfort in my ways or my words. I hated her hopelessness. I hated her cynical view of life. And most of all, I hated myself for not leaving her.

177

All through my story with Jackie, I was hurting and smashing against her resistance, her demands. But I thought that was marriage, normal. I thought the struggle was necessary to get stronger for almost 20 years, but Shamanic healings showed me a different perspective. Being alive sometimes means hurting, feeling sensations like pain. I never liked being numb. I wanted all the feelings that came with Love, even the hurt. I chose that life. Somewhere deep inside, I confused being treated poorly as a prerequisite for love. Humans are resilient, yet fragile. I signed up to be ignored and hated not being seen or heard. When I was so small and invisible in my family, I had nothing to offer my kids. No voice. But life force energy—or something else universal— showed me a more positive way to look at relationships, even the hurt, and the struggle. It's all temporary, except connections to other people. Connections are vital for love, but I had forgotten that I was part of the connection. I had forgotten that I count! I'm important, too! I was so busy trying to save Jackie and change her or support her. Neither of us loved ourselves or forgave ourselves enough to give love away. It's never about only one person. Every family member is important. I don't believe in hierarchy. My path and my lesson were to learn to love my kids and myself. Without that, I had nothing.

Part 5: Freedom

Freedom is the power or right to act, speak,
or think as one wants without hindrance or restraint.

Puking in the Bushes

Puking is to emit something (energy)
in an uncontrolled stream or flow.

Between the Reiki classes and the healings, I was in pursuit of Love. Adding more love into my life. One clear evening, I was so mad at how Jackie was acting. She was treating me like a child. I can't recall the content or argument. I was changing inside, but she wasn't. Pushing through the screen door, leaping off the stairs to outside, the stars seemed to stare at me, like they knew more about that evening than I did. I ran further into the yard and looked up again. Tingling went up and down my body, like jumping off a cliff, not caring if I lived or died, courage filling my chest, and then I yelled one corny line up to the starry sky, to God and to everyone who might listen, like Jodie Foster in the movie *Contact*, "I'm OK to go! I'm OK to go!" *God, please exist and get me out of this. If intentions truly count, and dreams can come true, then let me leave this home and gain more Love than ever before. Love, remember love.* I turned towards the house, still hoping for some attention. Through the window I saw Jackie walking around unassuming. She wasn't looking for me. She wasn't worried about me. She didn't realize she had treated me like shit. She probably didn't even pay attention to how she was treating me that night. Her priority was picking up the toys!!! Where was her concern about ME? Where was her kindness? Where was the love, the connection? Where was her compassion? I was ready to leave. I had tried everything, everything. Several years of changing my actions and going to therapy and still it felt like suffering. The suffering kept getting worse. No more suffering. Raising my chin up, seeing stars, I arched back, opened my arms up to the sky, surrendered control, and said many, many times, "I'm OK to go! I'm OK to go!" I was ready to leave the home with my kids and my wife for some better sort of life. I had no voice, no choice, no say, no power, barely any existence. I was dying and needed to save myself by admitting it was time to be brave and change. My kids needed me to be pure Alison. They saw me through Jackie's eyes, so they never saw *me* at all. It was time to step into a new role. I had to transform myself. I wholeheartedly let go of all my efforts to keep Jackie and Alison together. It was over. Over. It was futile.

Suddenly, something was surging through me. There was a shudder in my stomach. I dry heaved toward the orange tiger lilies. Whoa! This was happening!!! Part of me didn't believe it. Someone up there heard me and there was a process put in motion. There was pressure in my throat. I was suddenly puking in the bushes. Strangely, I was relieved and scared at the same time. Releasing all the guilt and anger and sadness, I quickly bee-lined back inside the house, went into the bathroom, and began to puke like I never puked before; for what seemed like hours. Holding the bowl like a buoy in the ocean, rising and falling on a ride of releases. At some point, Jackie leaned on the threshold and watched for a few minutes. She told me later it was too painful to watch the intensity and amount of puking. It was not a stomach bug. No one else got sick. It wasn't a coincidence. I vomited because I made a powerful wish. I was releasing all of the fears and doubts inside my body. It was an extension of the healings I'd done with Jade. It was deeper and further releases of anger. I had been stuffing down anger, stuffing down revenge, stuffing down all my pissed-off rants that I never aimed at Jackie. I closed my eyes the entire time, my head in the toilet bowl, crying, releasing intense negative energy and years of pent up fury and hurt. Jackie knew without me saying. We both knew I was changing. I was puking up all the past shit between us. Breaking a part was the only way to move towards being whole again.

A few days later, Jackie was asking me to watch "Hope Springs" starring Meryl Streep and Tommy Lee Jones. It was about a couple that grew apart over the years. They didn't seem to love each other anymore, but were trying to create a spark again. I couldn't even watch the whole thing. My gut felt weak. I asked her to stop the movie. It forced me to feel my own deadness inside, sick and hollow. Where was the passion? Where was the love? All the chemistry was gone between them, just like me and Jackie. They couldn't kiss! Their timing was so far off they bumped heads. I wasn't ready to view such a display of clumsiness, loveless, guarded, and distant relationship. "What did you think of that movie? What do you think of their relationship?" Jackie asked me the following night.

I couldn't believe she was bringing up that stupid movie

again! During the movie, my chest ached as I watched the couple struggling to talk about their issues and spill their feelings in front of a therapist. They seemed miserable and so terribly lonely. The similarities to us were astoundingly obvious. I was afraid to admit how 'done' I was with Jackie. I didn't want to have any responsibility for lost love. I didn't want to see myself portrayed in that movie, but I did. I spent the evening trying to change the subject. Sitting up straight and facing me on the couch, Jackie clearly seemed to want to know my thoughts about it, but I dodged her for as long as I could. Eventually, she asked again, "Do you think it was a true to life movie or not? Do you think they could grow back together?" I admitted that it's hard to have hope in a marriage that far gone.

"Why?" Jackie asked curious. "Do you think it's not worth saving their marriage?" as if she objected.

"No, I think every couple's different, but sometimes if the trust is lost, then staying together and trying to love again is too hard to do. For me, if I don't feel safe, then it's too hard to be intimate. I can't be vulnerable if I don't feel safe. And if I can't be vulnerable, then I can't truly, fully love. To me, loving is being intimate, open, and vulnerable with your partner." I couldn't believe we were having this conversation so casually. It was surreal. Yet we weren't truly talking about us, we were talking indirectly about us.

"That couple had their guard up too long. I think their guard will most likely stay up, so they won't ever love again. At least not each other," I added, looking down at my hands.

For the first time in many years, she listened to me. She responded by inquiring further about my feelings for her. I very gingerly said, "I think people change and want different things after many years together. I always told you we had to work on self-growth first, but that's not helping us. We've been in therapy." Her eyes stayed on me while I spoke. She looked down at her hands and nodded. Maybe she was ready to hear me. Maybe she ached for resolve.

Sitting in our living room, our discussion kept on going, in an earnest tone. We calmly talked about all the ways we had tried to stay together and how nothing was working. "Remember when we first started seeing Deb?" I asked. Deb was our couples' therapist for 8 years. "Yes," she said, looking out the window. "Did you think it helped?" I asked. She hesitated, "I guess not. Not really.". "Neither of us are adapting or changing any longer! Yet we still try to change each other!" I said. Finally, I dove at the chance to say, "Maybe we should just take a break and see how separating goes. I think I should move out for a while." I was dying for any way out I could find. Especially now, because this was the first time she wasn't emotional! She had a steady, pensive gaze when she looked at me and listened. Her eyes blinked slowly, as her head nodded slightly as I spoke. There were no distractions, no tasks, and no children interrupting. We actively listened that evening.

"OK." She sighed deep, "You could move out and we can see if that helps us." But she never remembers saying this. From this very moment on, she blamed me. I should have suspected, but I was honestly surprised that from that moment on, she always said it was my idea to leave and separate. She never remembered this conversation again. She made herself the victim.

Two days later, her anger kicked in. "I'll give you six weeks to find somewhere else to live!" She kicked me out of the bedroom that night. "You can sleep on the upstairs screened-in porch." She told me. Yes, the porch where we were married. The kids had no idea I was sleeping out there. The porch was never insulated. It had ripped up paint, no flooring, lopsided walls, half glass and half paneled. At night the foxes in the woods sounded like screaming women or ghosts. It was cold and creepy, but where else would I go? I couldn't leave. I couldn't stay. Each night, I sat on the mattress rocking and crying, my arms around myself. Aching, thinking she wanted to punish me. I was frozen there, at that house. I was so scared to leave. It felt completely wrong to leave my kids home. I couldn't do it. Filled with fear, I delayed and delayed until she set down that deadline of six weeks, whereupon I decide to fix up the barn on our property. I could live there. Why would I want to live next to Jackie? But I wanted to share the yard with my kids. I thought it was genius! It had electricity in it, all I needed was plumbing and heating. No problem. And then the estimates came in for the cost of plumbing and heating that barn, then my idea to live in the barn, went down the drain.

Again, I wondered... *where am I going to stay?* I was terrified. Jackie might have been an obstacle, but she was my home. She was my family. It killed me to leave her, leave my kids, leave my Sienna-pup. I tried to backpedal. I wanted to stay at that house. I had no desire to actually go through with anything. *Could I change my mind?* My parents and siblings were in Pennsylvania. I didn't have any friends to live with. Jackie took care of so many parts of the house and the stuff! *How would I adjust?* I didn't think I could learn or adapt to these changes. I pictured myself in a gutter on the side of the road, alone. I started to lose myself in a dark abyss of fear. *Where will I live? What can I do for security?* I saw no future, no hope. I was trapped under my fear, paralyzed by my lack of choices.

Some of my friends at work were 'sort of' offering their homes temporarily, but not really. All of them were worried about me, my lack of options, but none of them wanted me to live with them, even temporarily. I didn't want to be a burden to anyone. Around that same time, I met a new colleague named Karel and asked her to lunch. We were standing in the hallway, headed back to our offices, when I did something I don't usually do. "Wanna go to lunch?" I asked as I walked away. "Yeah," she said, "that sounds fun." Karel was quirky and bold, around my age but didn't know anyone. She was a scientist who supported other women in the workplace. She spoke her mind, but still asked about my opinions. As I picked her up for lunch, we laughed when we realized we owned the exact same red Honda CRV. The Thai restaurant was pastel orange inside. We sat by the window and watched people walk by on the sidewalks. As we ate spicy peanut noodles, she told me she moved to Connecticut from upstate New York alone into a beautiful, big house with four bedrooms. "So there's plenty of room for overnight guests," she laughed, making fun of herself. Apparently, her friends from out of state often stayed over for a few nights. I was jealous. I didn't have close friends I visited with anymore. Suddenly, I only wanted to chat about light topics, plus neither of us wanted to go back to work.

Back at my cubicle, I confided in my close friend Erin about my lunch conversation with Karel. She got big eyes and said, "Problem solved! She has four bedrooms! Ask Karel to rent a room. Then you won't be a burden on your friends. You'll get a space of your own and give her money for it. It's a win-win." About a week later, I worked up enough nerve. I texted Karel, "What do you think if

I rent a room from you for a few months while I find a place to live?" She texted me, "That might work for me." The next day, she called me and said yes and invited me to see her place. I drove over after work to see her spare room. It was absolutely perfect, in the woods, quiet, and close to work. She lived on a dead end road; all gorgeous homes with trees surrounding. The double-garage made me beam as I pulled down her incredibly steep driveway between two pine trees. The garage was in the basement, then up a flight of stairs to the kitchen and living room with a large deck, canopied by tree limbs. Up another flight to my potential bedroom, it had its very own bathroom. *Jackpot! My OWN bathroom and shower!!* The floors were pine with huge windows and a small deck through the slider doors. It had a double bed and a great view of the forest. Karel's room was up the last flight on the floor above. I never went up there. She named it the Queen's tower and cackled as she sipped tequila. The only person who objected to my moving in was Karel's dog. The dog considered my room, her room. So I adapted by letting her lounge on my bed most of the days I was at work or with my kids. I offered Karel a fair rent and she accepted.

Locks

Locks are used to make an object
rigidly fixed or immovable.

I rehearsed, I practiced, I memorized, I wrote notes, but nothing prepares you for the first time you tell your kids you are moving out and leaving them to live with one parent. Prior to the family meeting, Jackie said that it was my decision to leave her. She forgot her threats to kick me out. Through her teeth she said, "You have to tell them, since this is what you want, not me."

As I started to talk with Noah and Maria, I knelt down in front of them, tears in my eyes, hands shaking. Both kids were confused and sad and scared. I glanced over at Jackie between sentences. She was okay, very calm, some tears in her eyes too, but she almost looked as though she liked the stress and suffering in that moment. Part of me wanted her to help me, to save me, to save us, to stop me, to do something loving, but she didn't. Noah was sitting on the couch, short legs stretched out in front of him, so small and innocent. Maria was leaning on the arm of the chair, visibly aware that something bad was coming out of my mouth. *I can't do this. I'm not strong enough*. Maria didn't like my tears. She knew something was wrong. I ached. My heart was pounding and breaking and my throat was swelling. Jackie tried to reassure them. I was unraveling, falling to my knees, looking at the floor, fighting back tears, but everything got blurry—it was no use.

As I prepared to present to them my main points of separation and living somewhere else, I figured less was more—don't say too much. But my points felt idiotic, empty. "Sometimes families live in separate places. Ma is going to live somewhere else from now on. I'll still see you guys on Tuesdays, Thursdays, and one day of the weekend. It will *not* be much different. Ask questions, OK?"

Those were my five sentences. They were sustaining words for me to cling to as I bobbed in rushing waves of emotions and dread. Seasick. But it's just too, too, massive to digest for a kid who needs and deserves both their parents to raise them together. Noah nodded a lot and grinned with his bright little teeth, but his eyes stared at my tears. His body shrunk smaller, hoping to end the moment. He usually talked nonstop. Now he was silent, blinking back tears, checking our faces.

Maria moved and bent and arched and leaned on the couches. She wanted to run and hide, but she didn't. She kept fake-smiling and saying "it's going to be the same?!?!" We kept reassuring her that I'm not leaving them for good. I was still planning on being with them every other day, but I had no idea how.

Both kids were hurt, scared, confused, and broken. It seemed like a hole was widening in my chest. Like a tremor moving left and right under my feet, unsteady, unsure. If I could have turned back or undid it, I would have… for them. It felt so wrong for them, and yet right for me. I never felt so selfish.

Jackie had decided I had to leave that very same evening after telling the kids. She said it was less confusing, but I didn't agree at all, yet again, I didn't fight her. I should have stayed and listened to my intuition, but I acquiesced again. Poor Maria was heartbroken I left that same night. And I had stopped sleeping there for months until I could find a home for the three of us to be together. After I left, Jackie reported to me that Maria sat in the tub that night, sobbing, "You should have told me!" Unprepared for all these decisions and splitting apart the two people she loved so dearly. She was in shock at the news of my leaving. I created a doorway out and hated how it felt to walk through it.

Every time I left that house, each night I drove away for over a year, Noah hung out the front window and yell "Goodbye Ma! I love you Ma! See you soon Ma!" My heart ripped, ached, and burned inside and the road blurred with tears. Sobbing, I drove to my little room at Karel's, an hour south to sleep alone, to cry alone, to weep and write. It still hurts to remember, even now, but it's still a better life for all of us. The hurt isn't always with me, it fades once we see each other again. It grew much easier as the routine of seeing Noah and Maria every other day became solid and reliable and they could count on it too. Each time I showed up again at Cherry Street, they knew I didn't leave them. They trusted me. I never missed a day, even in bad weather.

That same day I told them, and the first evening I left my home and my kids, I intentionally planned to attend a Reiki share for an hour then travel south to Connecticut to Karel's room. It was a Sunday and I cried a ton in the parking lot of the Reiki Share. I cried in the car. Step by step, I slowly put one foot in front of the other toward the Reiki Share. I stopped on my way, leaning on the wall, and crying in the hallway. *Oh God, please help me!* I'd think. Again I'd take a step and lean on the wall, crying and weak. *What am I doing? What am I doing?* I'd whimper to myself. Getting my body into that Reiki share was my goal, even though being social or being with strangers was the last thing I ever wanted at that moment. Staying composed was a family gift. Looking calm, cool, and collected my forte. However, tonight, I wanted to just go lie down and bawl and bawl and curl up and cry and cry, but somehow, I opened the door and fell into the arms of my hospice coordinator, Remy.

"I left my family tonight!" I cried.

She took a deep breath and looked into my eyes and said "You didn't leave your kids. You left an unhealthy situation. Love all the parts of yourself!"

I heard myself gasping and felt myself shaking from crying so hard.

Love all the parts of yourself! Love all the parts of yourself!

Remy motioned for me to lie on the table first, before anyone. Shaking, I lay on the table, looking up at the ceiling. Oddly, eight Reiki practitioners were there. That was twice as many as usual. Peaceful, loving Reiki friends were offering positive energy. Tears were streaming down my face as I received all that Love for the first time in many, many years. Closing my eyelids, I saw hands and colored hearts. I trusted the people there. My breathing slowed down. My shoulders eased. I let them reach out to me and offer Love with nothing to offer back in return but tears and thanks. *Thank God*, I thought. *Thank God for that Reiki share*. It was a place to go.

When people don't know how to leave their abusers, they need a supportive place to go. They want friends to hold them without judgment, with no words, no advice, no criticism, no great ideas—only love. Friends need us to just be present. By their mere presence, I was supported. Did it make me feel better? You better believe it! Unconditional love—I soaked it up for all thirty minutes.

Until then, I had never trusted anyone enough to let them help me in my adult life; I had lacked trust and faith in others. Now, when I allowed myself to be helped and surrender my control, my heart began to blossom. Not only did it open me up to more possibilities, but the reciprocity caused a two-way type of unconditional Love flow. As risky as it felt to expose myself, the act of allowing someone to help me healed me. It enabled me to be vulnerable and trusting.

In my silence of receiving Reiki, I heard these sentences in my mind: *We are more than just bodies and minds. We are spirits. Energy allows the quiet wordless space for us to just BE and accept without intelligence or knowledge. Just by breathing air, by simply being... we are enough. Doing is not the only way to accomplish. Self-reliance, faith, courage, focus, connection, introspection should be acknowledged and valued too. Don't judge. Believe in yourself. Sing your own song. Plan your own goals. Listen to your own inner voice.*

The thoughts were acknowledging my irrefutable need to simply be, to live my life defined by my values, to be free. Now my telecommuting days were dedicated time with my kids. It meant driving an hour up to Jackie's. One time I got there early. It was snowing and freezing outside, which is why I was there early. She greeted me at the door and said I was two minutes early, go wait in the car. I waited in the car, angry.

On Tuesdays and Thursdays and Saturdays, I spent the day with Noah and Maria and then put them to bed until Jackie got home. Then I left around bedtime. If it snowed, I used to sleep at my friend Blair and Amy's. They lived 4 miles away from my kids. Snowing really hard, I was with the kids at Jackie's as it piled to 10 inches. I could stay at Blair's if I couldn't drive an hour south. It was slippery, but I had so much more faith now. I wasn't scared like I used to be in snow storms. But as the snow got deeper, Maria told Jackie I should be able to stay and sleep over. But Jackie decided no. After I put Noah to sleep, I went downstairs and strode to the opposite side of the house, away from her energy. As I looked out the window, she came up behind me. "You can't stay here," she said, standing as broad as she could in the dining room. She wanted to say so much more. "I'm a good person!" she said as tears started, "I'm a good person!" I held silent as she cried and turned away.

I went upstairs and said goodnight to Maria before heading out. As I put my coat on, Jackie talked with Maria and said goodnight, she came downstairs and said, "I don't want you here, but I'll let you stay this one time, because it will make Maria feel better. Unlike you, I put my kids first!" Maria was only 8 and she had more compassion than her mother. Jackie threw me a sleeping bag and said, "I'm not happy about this idea!" I was so sick of her acting like I had control of the snow, I yelled back, "It's not safe. You shouldn't be so stubborn!!" She flared, "Me?! You're the one who's stubborn! I'm the responsible one. We can't all go off chasing our dreams! You did this to us! I hope you're happy!" She turned on her heel and strode away.

I slept there, one last time on my former living room floor. I snuggled up to Sienna as much as I could. During the night, I had a nightmare that a queen bee kept stinging me in the mouth. I couldn't speak. It was stinging my hands and my mouth over and over again.

During this same time, I exercised my Reiki skills by volunteering for hospice. Helping elders passing away was one of the many ways Reiki could offer comfort. After all, it's one of my worst fears, dying. Why not offer a pain-free relaxing energy to ease the transition out of our bodies? Especially for those elders who have no one to be with near the end of life. I saw firsthand, the power of loving energy. As I entered the room, a reserved man was sitting, reading the paper next to his wife. She was unconscious and very obese. He was attentive and kind as I introduced myself, "I'm Alison. I'm going to offer your wife some Reiki if that's OK with you." He stood up and nodded. Quietly, he kept his eyes on me and then quickly stood and turned to lay down his paper on the chair. As I walked around her, I put my left hand on her shoulder and my right hand on her arm. He mirrored me on the other side of her and we both bowed our heads down and took a deep breath. We stood there in silence for 30 minutes or more, keeping our hands on her. Offering her Reiki was like praying. We were touching her softly without expectations, without words. Each of us noted our breathing, our intentions. We held her in light in our imagination. There was silence, yet mutual efforts. I left and he thanked me. She passed away later that night.

It was a Friday and I was driving back North to see my kids and I realized my check was going to be deposited into my account. Pulling up to the bank, the screen said, "not a valid account". Jackie had closed the account without telling me. Then when I went to the house to see Maria and Noah the doors were locked. My key didn't work. I knocked and knocked and finally, Sienna and the kids crowded to the door to let me in. "Mama changed the locks on the doors," Maria told me sadly. "She says she doesn't trust you."

"What do you think of that Maria?" I asked. "Do you think I would steal something?"

"No, but Mama thinks you shouldn't be able to come in our house anymore."

"Does that make sense to you? What can I do if I need to get your stuff for dance?" I asked Maria.

"I don't know. Mama didn't like that you came in the house one time without asking her," she quickly answered. Maria didn't want to discuss it. I was putting her in the middle.

Sneaking in to see Sienna was my main reason for wanting to get into Cherry Street. Seeing Sienna became increasingly difficult. I used to walk her on the bike path because she liked it, but Jackie said she was too old to be walked and it hurt her hips. I didn't walk her far and she loved it. After I left, I asked if I could walk Sienna since I was around, but Jackie said no. Being locked out meant I couldn't feed her either. Jackie would only feed her a can of dog food a day and she was a large 70 pound lab. She insisted Sienna stay skinny. I admit, I used to sneak in the house sometimes to give Sienna extra treats and food to keep her happier. Sienna was such an anxious dog, the fat in the food helped her. Each night I left the kids at bed time, I'd press my face against the picket fence and hold Sienna's fuzzy face to mine. I'd breathe her in slowly, smelling her essence, her dog scent. I loved Sienna with every cell inside me. She leaned against the fence too and panted and then licked my nose. We understood each other in a deep and loving place. I could feel that she wouldn't live much longer. She lived a few more years. Although I saw her less, I did get to visit her and press my forehead to hers from time to time.

For Noah's birthday party, Jackie set up his fourth birthday party at an ice skating rink. This event was more of a big deal than I would have choosen. In fact, she texted me the event was happening, but insisted later that she had asked me for my opinion. When I arrived the feeling was awkward. The other parents stayed away from me. Most of our mutual friends knew I had left the house five months ago, so they had plenty of sympathy for Jackie. None of them looked at me. A few of them hugged and kissed her when they arrived with Noah's friends. They all went out on the ice and skated. After, we went upstairs to the party room that Jackie had booked. She brought a cake and pretzels and popcorn for the kids. Some other snacks were brought and contributed by some other parents. I brought a gift for Noah and some lemonade as well. In all, there were about ten other kids enjoying the ice skating. I spent most of my time alone on the bleachers ignoring Jackie, but it was a little sad to be separated parents for Noah and Maria at our first big child event. Maria seemed to cling to me more, torn between friends and me being alone. She skated around with her friends, but kept glancing at me up through the party room glass from down on the ice. She was sensitive to both her mom's feelings. As I slowly made my move towards the exit, I grabbed Noah and told him I had to go. I gave him a squeeze. Quick as lightning, Jackie made her way out to the hallway where the exit was, "We have to pay them before we go."

"What? Who?" I said dumbstruck. This was the first time she spoke to me the whole party.

"Can you write the people a check for the party?" she asked. She was looking down at her shoes.

"What?" I said again, my eyes bulging. By then, the people at the register were staring at us. One of them said, "It costs one hundred and twenty dollars minus the deposit you put down for the room. That's ninety-five for today."

I looked at Jackie who was looking at the kids inside the rink. I was getting weak. I was giving her thousands of dollars monthly for child support. Now, I wasn't sure I could say no in front of my kids and these people. *Should I pay? Was I supposed to pay? Why should I pay?* Slowly my brain said, *No way!* Finally, I blurted out, "I don't have any money with me," then laughed weakly. "I'll contribute, but I'm not paying the whole thing!" I said too loud. People were staring at me. She grabbed her wallet from her coat in a huff and started to pay them. "I knew it! I knew it! I paid for rental skates! I brought the cake and the snacks! I knew it! Just so you know, no one likes your new idea that being selfish is a good way to be!" she said looking me straight in the face.

Punching her flashed across my mind. I turned and pushed hard on the rink door, both my kids chasing behind me. "Ma! Ma! Where are you going?" They saw we were bickering. They were afraid we would fight.

The walk to my car cooled me down a little. "It's OK, I'm OK, I'll see you guys tomorrow," I told them. I hugged them each in the parking lot as Jackie angrily unlocked her car for them to climb in. They didn't take their eyes off me as they drove away in her car.

Connecting to Others

Connecting is to join together or bring into contact
so that a real or notional link is established.

During all these major changes in my life, I signed up for a meditation class. Life was still stressful in many ways. Jackie hadn't let up much on me. At work, Jade and Erin and I meditated during lunch. We went to Erin's office, or walked out to the pond to meditate. The meditation was helpful for relieving my tension and finding answers and raising my vibration. I needed more practice. I wasn't good at it. Meditation had been something I was told to do forever but I never tried.

My psychic, Iva was offering a meditation class to help connect to Spirit and energy. This was my first time taking a meditation class. I was very nervous yet excited. I was much more comfortable because my friends, Erin and Lauren were joining me. The meditation class was a 2 hour class, every Monday for 6 weeks gathering at Iva's basement. I had gone to see Iva twice over the last 2 years, but only for readings, not classes. "Vee vell begeen wit thee cards!" she announced in her thick Polish accent. "Zee cards tell you your future!"

Iva began each class with an altar in the middle of the room. We picked 4 or 5 tarot cards each from the angel or guide cards. Then we went around the room to talk about how the cards resonated with us and how our goals were related to the cards. Iva began by making us move the energy. She blasted the music and we danced, banging on the floor with our legs, in a circle. She yelled, "What do you want in your life!?!?! Go get it!!! What do you want to say to your boss!?!? Tell him, 'fuck off' and get what you need in your life!!" We shook our bodies and tapped on our thighs and faces as she directed. Then she settled us down for a meditation or exercise. "First we move energy, then we open to the message to receive them," she said. Relaxing music played as she guided us through a meditation. Usually the meditation involved relaxing or letting go of stress from the head to the toes or through each chakra. Then she guided us to see loved ones and ask questions or ask for gifts to be handed to us. Each class was different with a wonderful combination of different cultural rituals and techniques for moving energy. The room was dimly lit, filled with blankets and pillows, it was warm and comfortable. It felt intimate and safe and she called on many diverse cultures to teach us to release and move negative energy out and open up to let in positive energy.

In one exercise, I sat cross-legged opposite my energy partner and visualized a thick stream of light and energy going from my heart to her heart. My partner was Iva, so I was very nervous. *Could I do this stuff? Could I send energy?* I did send energy for Reiki, but this was not Reiki, it was using your imagination, not hands, no touching. The music helped because it was perfectly chosen, making for a dramatic and soothing background. My eyes were closed the whole time. Slowly, I focused on sending golden and white light in a strong stream, like water going into Iva's chest. Suddenly my heart was vibrating and truly jiggling in my chest, side to side. We did this exercise for about 3 to 5 minutes. Afterwards, we shared our sensations and experiences during the exchange of energy. Iva said "I saw and felt how powerful you are!!" She said shaking her fist for emphasis. She then said, "I felt my heart….. jiggling in my chest. It was very powerful!!" She used the same phrase, "jiggling in my chest," that was exactly the thought in my mind during the exercise. Sending energy through visualization was real and true and could be experienced and felt by both the giver and the receiver. In that exercise, a woman sent flowers in her mind, and the receiving partner saw the flowers in her imagination. We went around the room and everyone saw or sensed the sending of energy, either through tingling or heat or other images they saw in their minds. Reports of common visions and experiences began to validate my confidence in energy medicine.

Sounding meant hollering out energy. In a sounding exercise, Iva made each of us stand in front of the class and sing your name out loud…one at a time. "Energy comes through voice!!" she said, chanting with gusto at me, "Al-ee-sun!! You will be a teacher! So say who you are!!! Like zees….. IIIIIIIIIIIIII aaaaaaammmmmmmmm Aaaaaaalllllleeeeeeesoooooooooooon!" in a monk type tonal voice, holding each vowel sound so I repeated her chant. Terrified, my voice broke and stayed quiet as I tried to chant aloud. Each time, she told me to say it louder. I did it six times, each time, feeling freer with each announcement. It was empowering to break through the fear of my own voice. It released the tension, similar to Reiki class, but more sensational, more movement of energy.

Another very poignant exercise was looking into each other's eyes. We all stood in two lines facing one another. We held hands with our partners and stared into each other's eyes. The gaze was held for about 3 or 5 minutes. It felt like forever, but you were not to break the gaze. You were again to feel the other person's energy. "Zee eyes are zee windows to zee heart!" Iva announced. As we began, I was struck by how hard it was to keep eye contact and how different each person's energy felt to me. "Don't hold back the tears. Let it all go!" I heard Iva saying behind me. I didn't feel like crying, but it was difficult, uncomfortable in my mind. The first woman had dark brown eyes and we settled into each other's eyes with only a bit of discomfort. She felt steady, but present. Kind, and even. The next woman seemed empty and hiding. She was harder to stare at because she was uncomfortable. Another woman, Judy was shaking and terrified. Her hands shook, her fingers were almost electric with energy and tremors. Then Iva said, "Did everyone stare at each other?" I hadn't gotten to the only two people I knew in class, Lauren and Erin. "No, I didn't get to everyone!" I said to Iva as everyone else stayed quiet. Lauren was first. I could tell she felt scared, exposed. "We can do this, my friend," I said out loud. She kept smiling, a big deliberate grin, but then her dark eyes welled up with tears, even as she kept smiling the whole time. I saw her fear. I witnessed her rawness, her exposure and tried to comfort her without words.

Last in line was my friend Erin. She felt familiar and I was a bit nervous about feeling exposed to her. I could see myself in her. Like me, I saw her steady determination. I observed her kindness, her desire to please, her open spirit. Erin's light blue eyes were endless, earnest eyes, soulful. There was a mirror quality to Erin, like she was me and I was her. We were the same height, so she felt comfortable and deeply good. I could sense her familiar spirit inside but also I could see safety and love. We settled in to each other nicely, naturally.

The entire exercise was so moving, so intense, almost, life-altering. There was some realization inside myself about our likenesses and our differences. We each were vulnerable, yet guarded. Each wanting to end the vulnerable exercises, yet show that we were "good enough." I experienced our duality of loving yet wounding. The energy provided the link that wouldn't be there if we weren't together, being open. A mutual letting-down of our guard happened in those brief moments of vulnerability. Each exercise helped me feel less afraid of other people, all people.

Iva announced to the class in her strong Polish accent, "We are all CO-nnected!" Seeing into each other's eyes brought that connection out more, accentuated it. This type of exercise provided more physical proof and more sensations to truly experience and feel our connection, our need for each other.

These classes and Reiki and healings with Jade gave me several different spiritual tools to work with and to grow during this separation. I was beginning to get a hold of the person that I wanted to become! My belief that I didn't deserve to be happy was fading. My belief that I was a crappy mom and a crappy wife was dissolving. It was me who held those beliefs. It was me who was blocking my true self from arriving and showing up. I was so afraid and anxious, that I had built a life around fighting Jackie rather than stepping into my own beliefs about myself. It's a risk to take on all the responsibility of your own life. There's no scapegoating. There's no more excuses. I had built up the courage to leave my situation. Apparently, I was a much stronger person than I had ever thought to believe.

During one of the first meditations, Iva sat cross legged on a pillow by the music and guided us as we laid on our backs on the floor in pillows. She led us through the meditation, "zee color red is vashing down our bodies vith each breath from our crown chakras down to our toes", describing each body part being covered in the red as it washed down our bodies. She went through red, then did the same washing over visualization for orange, yellow, green, light blue, indigo, and finally purple. As we lay deeply relaxed and listening, Iva told us to visualize our most 'beloved' coming to us with gifts. I heard the woman next to me snoring. Tender waves of emotion washed over me as I saw my children bringing me gifts of love and affection. They were older, taller than me and hugging me. My kids were my greatest teachers, but I kept telling myself that I wasn't a good enough Ma. I began to believe in the softening of my fears into love. I hadn't allowed myself to enjoy my kids. I made parenting a chore, a task. I tried too hard to be perfect in my parenting. I wasn't nearly as authentic as I wanted to be with them. Opening was easing the tension of perfection. This meditation began to open my heart to allow them to teach me. My own guarded ego was keeping everyone at a certain distance. How could I love my children, if I didn't learn to allow them to love me too? It opened me. At the closing of class, a tarot card showed a mother and her two children reaching for each other with open arms. The card read, "Healing will come through your family". Miracles and messages came through Iva's meditations as well as her tarot cards. All I had to do was to listen.

The Tender Middle

Tenderness is showing
gentleness and concern or sympathy.

"As she learns to open her heart and be raw around them she will come to understand the love that will guide her wherever she may go" were the words that resonated with me from Ned's reading years earlier. I was learning to connect more deeply with my kids, but I still needed to find a space to share and raise my kids. Karel didn't like kids at her house, so they never came to my room in Connecticut. Prior to moving in, Karel was honest and told me she didn't want kids around her. But I traveled to my kids and used my former home as base until I found my own space. After all, Massachusetts was where their friends were, where their classes were, where their lives were located.

In seclusion, away from other people, I grew very comfortable at Karel's house. I did want to be with my kids, but I also knew this time by myself was what I needed to move forward. My heart ached at first, not being in the house with my dog and my kids.

Yet, I needed the recovery time to build strength. My soul had been broken down by Jackie. My sense of self was still connected strongly to her. Even the kids were repeating the same negative messages Jackie did, so I needed to protect myself from that toxic environment, or to at least break the cycle with some time away for respite. It was simply space and time to re-establish myself and recover from years of verbal abuse. My friend Gloria gave me credit and said, "Not for nothing, but you've never missed one day with those kids, come rain, sleet, or snow." I found the strength to still drive to my former home every other day, and every weekend to watch their events or drive them to activities. My ultimate goal was to recover first, then find a new home for us to begin again.

Meditating, writing, walking in the woods, eating healthy, resting, sleeping well, I lived closer to work, so I had an easier commute. My room had a sliding door out to a beautiful view on the third floor overlooking the thick pine woods. I saw birds and foxes and heard the wind through the trees. Karel was kind and accommodating and let me have privacy or asked to socialize if I wanted. Sometimes she had friends over to visit. Always allowing me the room to recover and remained non-judgmental. Many times, I stressed out about finding an apartment, except I tried to have Faith, but what is Faith? Do I do nothing? Do I pray? What will bring me what I need? I spent a lot of time trying to simply stay present and get through each day, each night. I quit drinking because I was afraid I'd be drunk all the time. I tend to love to numb out in stressful times. I lost weight, dropping from a size 8 to a size 4. There's no appetite in break ups. There's less joy in eating. I was recovering from leaving my "goal" life of having a family, a wife and two kids. It's exposing to admit you want to break a family up, vulnerable. A wallflower by nature, I didn't like affecting anyone and this was affecting everyone I loved. The Alison I had imagined had changed dramatically. Who did I want to be?

Being raw and open around my kids was still very difficult for me. I was raw in a way that exposed my emotions a little more, revealing my honesty and my mistakes. For instance, ants appeared on my living room floor one day. I said, "Noah, you can't just shove crumbs off the couch onto the floor!" He stopped and looked at my face and responded, "Ma, YOU brushed them off the couch yesterday!" Rather than denying and trying to be right, I listened to him. Remembering he was exactly right, I sulked a little and said, "You're right Noah. I'm sorry I blamed you. I forgot I did that. I was trying to show you to clean up yesterday and I showed you the wrong way. Now we have ants. Let's both try to vacuum rather than brush the crumbs onto the floor, OK? Maybe we can avoid the ants." I admitted I didn't show him the right thing and joined him in the correction. It was raw because it was difficult for me to slow my reactions down enough to hear and listen and then admit my errors all in a split second to a small child. In the past, I would have just reacted without thinking.

Because of our household habits, they were still in a power struggle with me often. "That's what you get!" Noah said, as he grabbed the rug off the kitchen floor and shook it with all his might to deliberately make a dusty mess at me. He was making his point, echoing Jackie's words and actions, already, as young as 3 years old. *Don't mess with me or I'll ruin your stuff.*

I blamed myself more and more for their bad behavior. I figured they never really even needed me in their lives, but one day

Noah and I were in the middle of playing Candyland, when he said, "Ma, you know when you go stay with your friend at her house? I really hate that." He meant going to Karel's house didn't make sense to him. As we continued playing the board game, tears welled up in my eyes. Then Maria told Jackie one day, while protesting and yelling about her hair issues, "I hate when it's only one mom!" It killed me to make Maria sad.

I cried a lot at Karel's house, yet I also felt happier, more content. I was very grateful not to be living with Jackie. I definitely felt better away from her energy. And I could not help my kids while I was still living in the house with her. That wasn't making any of us happy. Although I missed having Love in my life—although love was almost enough to make me stay—I couldn't withstand the pressure and strain of my relationship with Jackie, or affecting my kids in such a negative way, with the tension, the hatred, the seething.

I wondered if the kids may actually have a better life without seeing me for 12 hour blocks of time. In a fury after I moved out, Jackie stung me with, "Let's face it, the kid's lives STALL when they're with you! I keep them going, keep them productive! They accomplish nothing with YOU!" I thought, *not being productive isn't stalling.* Life is a balance of doing and being. Doing and producing is not the meaning of life. Love is the meaning of life, which is with us no matter what we happen to be DOING! Because of rants like that, I wished Jackie was a little less in their day to day life. Parents can be part of a child's life, but not all of it. Kids need their independence from their parents. Jackie's wish was to protect the kids, guide them. "We should be the biggest influence on their lives, not their friends," she said. I'm not so sure about that. Not if Jackie saw the world as unsafe and scary and I viewed the world as trusting and loving. The two extremes were probably hard to navigate for Noah and Maria.

There was a big change for all of us with me living at Karel's. I drove to the house every other day to spend the whole day, from 7am to 7pm with the kids while Jackie worked, just as I always did. Except now I came from Karel's house and I didn't have to work anymore when I was with them. No longer split in time, trying to be in two places at once; work and home.

After a few weeks of living at Karel's, Jackie tried to convince me not to see Noah at bedtime after I moved out of the house, because he cried about missing me. "You can't put him to sleep anymore. It's too hard on him! He's crying all the time since you left here." Falling asleep he often cried, so did Maria at his age. Kids have lots of feelings. Jackie didn't want Noah's feelings hurt, so she protected him. But he never wanted me to leave ever. Transitions were hard for all of us, particularly for Noah since he's the youngest. It made him cry. But she forgot that he used to cry every night falling asleep. It was a way to release and surrender to sleep. She made everything about me, blamed me for anything bad or difficult.

My parents came up to support me during the separation. We all visited briefly at Jackie's. They were staying in a hotel, since I had no space for them at Karel's. Noah was too young to stay overnight at the hotel. But this one time, I did not leave the house without seeing Noah first. I did NOT listen to Jackie. He was so happy to see me. "Ma!!!" he said, hugging me with both arms and legs. As we embraced, he said, "I love you Ma! I love you with my whole heart!"

As I was putting on my coat to go to the hotel with Maria and my parents, I noticed sadness in him. He was all teary and choked up

211

because he wasn't coming with us. A voice in my head said, *Go to him. It's you he needs. Your love.* I stopped what I was doing, I became very present and sat down with him on the couch. I wrapped my arms around him. The love was tingling from my heart and radiating outward. It actually hurt a little; it ached in my chest. I sobbed as my tears fell, his fell too.

"I love you Noah," I told him.

"I love you too," he said. "Can't you stay? Why do you have to go?" he asked. "I'll be back in the morning. I understand why you don't want me to go. It hurts a lot. But we really are okay," I consoled him.

All that love between us, it was worth every ounce of hurt and pain in my chest, every bit of it. Sometimes people don't talk about it, the hurt, the tender middle, the familiar pain of love, but I think it's worth it. Because love keeps on going. It won't ever stop. I find that powerful! Love fills you so much at times, it truly aches. I hope adults don't model avoiding love to their kids. To me, feeling love is better than being numb.

As Noah and I hugged and cried, my mom and dad were at the door watching, crying with us, until Jackie swooped in, sat on the couch and tried to protect him from me. He was buried in two moms. She constantly misjudged the importance of me in their lives. In the moment of all of us crying, Noah started joking and laughing to lighten up the mood with, "I can't breathe under here people! Who turned out the lights?!"

I hope my kids feel the importance of loving and the peace of authenticity. Revealing my true self to adults and other older people, made me feel like a freak as a child. It grew more difficult to stand out and speak up. The brave and outspoken part of me slowly learned to keep quiet, fade back. They refer to it as domestication. My whole childhood was free and accepting when I was able to escape to the woods or with my neighbors. The wild child grew to hide. As I got into junior high, pretending to be someone else became more necessary as my norm. Hiding my tough and confident soul became my teenage job. I barely resembled my young, bold Alison. I was taught over and over to dress like a girl and act like a girl and people will accept you and like you for your beauty. "Don't be authentic" was my motto in new relationships. So I assumed the real me must not be very loveable. 'Not loveable' stuck with me.

When my kids came along, acquiescing to others squashed my attempts at being a good Mom. I guess I didn't know how to be truly all the diverse parts of my personality. I couldn't remember how to be me. Pretending didn't feel right. After the separation, I was amazed at how much my kids loved me without my having to pretend. I was not the star mother, but my kids loved when I played with them and paid attention to them. We shared our thoughts and told stories. I could see their eyes checking mine to be sure I was watching them. The more I watched, the closer we became and the more love grew between us. It was out of my hands. It was easier than I expected. Don't get me wrong, kids are messy and emotional, but when I listened to them, they listened better to me too. They taught me so much by their mere presence, by sharing space together and giving them my loving attention. One of the best traits I offered them was listening.

Intention

Intention is a course of action;
it is one's purpose or objective; a plan.

Wishing and intention turned out to truly help me get what I wanted in my life. I wanted to live in the woods. I wanted a garage for my car. I craved the quiet and the seclusion of the tall, tall trees. But, I also needed to live close to my kids. All the apartments I looked at were cold and cement and brick. I interviewed for rooms and rental apartments all around town. One woman offered me a small room filled with cat hair and the option to sleep with her for $400 (the cat, not the woman). It was not looking good. I prayed and asked the universe for a home similar to Karel's but close to Cherry Street. As I drove south after taking care of my kids, I drove by a FOR RENT sign to my left. It was a green rancher at the base of a mountain, a former ski area and now several acres of reserved woods behind the house. It had 3 bedrooms and a garage and overlooked the woods. It was expensive, but I could afford it. Maria and I walked through the house and she loved it! It was perfect for us; big backyard, an acre, three bedrooms, a garage, one floor, baseboard heat, huge empty basement, porch on the back with a slider door. We drove to the realtor and filled out an application and waited. About two weeks later they called me. I was chosen to rent the house! My wish came true! It had all the things I asked for. It wasn't a coincidence. Many people had applied for that quaint house on an acre of lawn. I could hardly believe that after ten months of living apart from my kids at Karel's house and driving to Cherry Street every Tuesday, Thursday and Saturday through snow, sleet, and ice, I would now be only a mile away from them. 'Not for nothing', I never missed one day of caring for my children.

On moving day, I sent a small moving truck to Jackie's house to pick up my boxes. Jackie had packed everything into the barn. There were over 40 boxes of my stuff that she had moved out of the house and into the barn from me to take away. It had been months of her slowly moving everything out of the house. My most prized possession was my treadmill. I couldn't wait to set it up in my cellar at the rental house only a mile away. It took very little to pay for the movers and move all the boxes to my new place, but when I opened them, they were mostly empty boxes, filled with trash and old bags. Almost everything in the boxes was junk or old yearbooks from my high school or memorabilia from before I met Jackie. None of my tools. No pictures of my kids. No kitchen utensils. None of the gifts she gave me for our 18 years together.

I mentioned it to Maria, "Seems like a lot of my stuff is out of your house." Because I was there every other day, I noticed. All my pots and pans and cookware were gone. All my favorite cutting boards and knives were gone. And all my weights and thera-bands were gone. All my anything was gone.

"Oh," Maria said, "we had a big yard sale one of the days in the fall after you moved out. We made a lot of money."

"Oh," I said, "that's good you made all that money." Jackie had sold everything and filled the barn with boxes of nothing. I couldn't believe it. I dropped the subject. Stuff doesn't matter as much as people do. And when I plugged in the treadmill, it didn't work. It never worked again.

Red Velvet Cape

Velvet is a closely
woven fabric.

After being separated for nine months, we finally found our new space. Jackie had bought me out of our Cherry street house we purchased together. In return, she asked me to pay off several of our credit cards, and I did. But eventually, after lots of arguing about money, I proposed to pay her $1000 each month as child support. I was incredibly grateful to receive the money for half of my house and create a living space in a rental house.

Now, in the new home, I was able to enjoy my kids with even more freedom. The kids and I established a beautiful slope to sled down in the winters. We made fairy houses in the woods. We ran through the sprinkler in the huge yard. Their faces were bright and smiling, like in a movie, as we checked every inch out of the new space. I had a yard with tons of woods behind it for exploring. We played badminton when my sister and her husband visited. The fire pit was fun for story-telling and roasting marshmallows when my brother and his wife visited. We made puppet shows in the cellar with my parents. I showed them how to play card games when they were bored. We watched movies and ate popcorn and loved our freedom.

We loved being together and laughing often. Slowly, I started to create my own, more relaxed rules. We didn't have to clean up all the time. They didn't have to worry about losing pieces to games. At first, it was a freefall of too many sweets and ice cream and too much technology or screen time. But slowly it didn't serve any of us to wreck my house. I sat with them and talked about how it felt to eat too much and watch too much and problem-solved together for how we might create specific rules to make us happier and connected.

I gave them choices for what to do with our time together. "The experts say that 2 to 4 hours is plenty of screen time. What times of the day do you think you'd like to reserve for watching?" I'd ask them.

"We like to watch right when we get here from Mama's house," they agreed.

"OK, but you can't watch the whole time you're here, so what about at the end of our time together?"

"We want to play Frisbee and monkey in the middle with you, but after we watch for an hour. And then we'll watch again, but leave our last hour to play with you." Maria suggested.

"OK, we'll start with two one-hour slots, but we have to follow the rules. And I'll write them on the whiteboard to help us remember. I'll call you when I'm ready to go outside."

"OK MA!!" they happily ran to watch for an hour. Usually out in the living room with headphones on or at the kitchen table, so I could see the screens and check on them.

That's how we created some rules to help guide our

technology. Not what's best for everyone else, but what's best for us. That was my new motto. Usually, we started to go over those times because I was on the phone or life disrupted our schedule, but I brought them together again and discussed it to re-establish the boundaries of watching. It wasn't easy. They did protest. But I began to lessen my anger about screen time. And when I get sick of the screens taking over, then I reset the rules and talk to them about it, rather than ranting and complaining. I'm in charge of the peace in my home. It took me a while to assert my style.

Another rule developed around losing tempers. I realized Noah was getting more and more angry and reacting faster and being more physical with me, so I asked my therapist for help and advice. She said to focus on eliminating the worst behavior first, which was using his hands or punching or kicking anyone, including me or Maria.

I sat the kids down again and asked them, "What do you think would help you when you're truly angry and you need to hit something?" They looked at me blankly, neither had answers. They knew it was bad to have that much anger, neither kids were modeled an appropriate resolution by their parents.

"Maria, the other day, you did the right thing, you ran into your room," I looked into her eyes. She looked surprised. "Yes, you and Noah were arguing and instead of punching or kicking, you ran into your room. That was excellent! You took care of you and didn't hurt Noah." With that in mind, I told them that running in your room and cursing or punching pillows in there was an acceptable way to let out your anger. Then a few days later, Noah screamed at me in the kitchen and tried to punch me. I walked past him to my room and shut the door. He tried to chase me in there and banged on the door, but I just stayed in there and didn't speak. He eventually found something else to do. The physical contact decreased dramatically over two weeks of consistently not reacting with more anger to anger. Walking away helped me stop using my hands on Noah and modeled some control for both Noah and Maria. Yelling and hitting became markedly less in my household. Less attention, diminished his behavior.

As we got toward the end of our long days together, I was relieved from the pressure I put on myself to parent better. I sort of let my hair down and cut loose. I wore a red velvet cape, a hat with tassels, and then blasted music and began to dance—something I had been doing since Maria was about two. I think she became a ballet dancer because of all the music we played and the dancing we did during all of our twelve-hour days together. Dance was a signal of peace, a momentary joy. It represented the ease of movement. It was a way to cope with life's stressors. Even after Noah was born, we put on dress-up clothes and choreographed dance routines in tights and tutus. Noah was often in Maria's leotard and flats with sequins and smiling in photos. It was chaotic but we had so much fun and we were free!

Cold Ma/Warm Ma

Cold lacking affection or warmth
of feeling; unemotional.
Warm is having, showing, or expressive
of enthusiasm, affection, or kindness.

Discussions and natural consequences were part of what helped my kids and me establish a new way of behaving and a new set of rules in my house. For example, one day, Maria and Noah begged me to go sledding down my backyard hill. They wanted me to join them, to play with them. It was icy and I was worried about their safety. They both kept telling me to relax and not to worry. Their inclination was to ride very fast down this white glaze of packed snow toward the busy road. To me, it made perfect sense that I could catch them at the bottom of the hill in front of the traffic, rather than them soaring into the busy road.

Maria went first, running and jumping on the plastic sled. Screaming toward me happily, she crashed into my waist and thighs. I caught her and the sled, but it left bruises on my legs. Noah went next. After a few runs, they began going even faster and I noticed I was lunging more toward them as they soared left to right at higher speeds to hit me. They swerved from the speed of the sled, causing them to seem unruly to stop.

The stupidest idea came from me. I suggested they get on together like my brother and I used to do. They excitedly hopped on full speed towards me. Noah got on Maria's back and they were screaming towards me down the hill. Swish, swish, left, right, faster, faster, faster....*holy moly, what if I can't stop them!* I braced myself. They smashed into me. Maria blasted against my stomach and Noah's solid skull crashed into my nose. *Crack!* I landed on my butt and saw black even with my eyes opened, then eventually I saw stars. "Ma? Ma? Ma?" Noah kept repeating. "Are you okay, Ma?" Both of them started laughing and rolling around on the snow. Under a circle of stars, I sat for a while to get my bearings, hands on my face. No blood. I couldn't see much. Crap, I was grumpy. My legs were aching and bruised. My nose was cracked. In a daze, surrounded by lots of ice, I stumbled into the house to get ice from the freezer. Parenting is painful. As the slider door shut behind me, I heard the kids laughing.

When I came back out, they were smiling at me. "That was so awesome! I thought you were dead!" Noah said with eyebrows up.

"Ma, you should have seen your face! You were like, *Whoa*! It was so, so, so fun!" Maria giggled. We had made a memory. We still tell that story.

Eventually, they started up again sledding, but they didn't go nearly as fast. I watched from the window. To adapt, they simply jumped or rolled off before they got to the road. Their natural survival instincts were much better than my idea of inserting myself into the path. I couldn't possibly control it. Either way, they were going to sled. But it wasn't helping to have me get hurt. I was interfering. So far, neither of them was going to slide into the road. They didn't go fast enough. But when I was standing there to catch them, they were full speed. Trusting I would be the strong parent who saved them.

We all have to save ourselves. I had to change myself. When my kids were born, my self-doubt as a parent fueled my family issues and fueled my suffering. I was guilt-ridden. I wasn't always consistent or understanding with my kids. My parenting skills needed work. I was scared of my kids! Thrashing and yelling and ordering them around wasn't getting them to act better or improving their behavior. What was I teaching them? It took time to figure out how I wanted things to go, what I wanted my relationship with them to look like. Push pull held me hostage. Push to be a good parent, pull to not have rules, to not be strict. I didn't want to be the "boss" or "in charge". Things improved when I wrote it down in my journal, things like, "I want peace in my house" or "I want to listen to my kids" or "I don't want anyone to hit each other". They were wishes for potential boundaries. Recording our progress in my journal helped also. Gradually, keeping them off technology made me less frustrated. My mood improved because we spent more time talking and playing together and less time with me telling them what to do. I resisted boundaries for so long. Once I chose the details of my boundaries, my angst subsided. My therapist helped me define my beliefs and boundaries. I was leading my kids to navigate our new household. Creating broader boundaries allowed Noah and Maria to explore more and make mistakes and not have me constantly reminding them of simple things like when to eat, when to go to the bathroom and when to brush their teeth. I watched them grow and learn by giving them more independence and freedom in their world, rather than intervening as much. I never liked micromanaging my kids. Jackie was incredibly controlling and I was determined to show my children another way. Boundaries felt more flexible for the good of everyone, and based more on safety, where rules seemed strict and rigid. It took time for me to set up boundaries, to see them as helpful guidance rather than binding and controlling.

All those changes occurring within the kids two worlds from our separation seemed to affect Maria the most. She wasn't used to so much decision making for herself. Often Maria felt like I ignored her because I wasn't micromanaging her actions. I wanted her free and independent, not codependent. Before our separation, Maria grew up with Jackie's way. Kids adapt to anything you give them. Jackie and I agreed over texts that Maria needed more support. Maria had a new propensity for grandiose storytelling around her friends, more crying at home, and signs of rebellion in the form of her wanting her iPod and sneaking it to bed around Jackie. I texted Jackie saying Maria clearly had anxiety when she first arrived here at drop offs. Then Jackie texted me also, saying transitions were difficult for both kids, especially moving continuously between our two houses. We decided to seek professional help through a therapist.

After several texts, Jackie and I agreed to get therapy together to try and support the kids in a healthy way, with objective guidance. Texting was a less than effective method to making big decisions concerning our kids' schooling, religion, money, friends, and many other issues. And our beliefs were opposing, we disagreed on everything. We needed a moderator. Jackie kept me out of almost every doctors' appointment and every decision about the kids. Maria's school didn't have my name until I went there myself and gave them my address and phone number. I thought seeing a therapist might help me be heard by Jackie as a parent. I did everything I could to find a third party to get Jackie to hear my ideas about the kids.

Finally, we sat down with a therapist, Sharon. We discovered Sharon had a unique therapy technique for releasing beliefs through tapping or emotional freedom technique (EFT). This type of therapist guides participants to focus on beliefs and then release them, much like the healings I had done with Jade and the techniques taught by Iva. The method was not talk therapy, although there was some discussion involved. The goal was to release energy and beliefs and triggers by touching the meridians of the body with your fingers and then announcing your intentions and emotions on specific issues, such as not wanting to be in charge of my kids or other held beliefs that weren't serving us.

Sharon was tall and confident. Her office was small on the third floor, she sat in a comfy chair with her knees bent, her feet up on the foot rest. Her eyes were sympathetically fixed on mine as I gripped my tissue. I cried about not knowing how to parent, not knowing how to help my kids effectively. I still doubted myself as a mom and was scared of my own kids. "I hate all their emotions. I wish they wouldn't explode at me! I try not to say no because of the huge reaction that comes back at me, sometimes it's violent and in my face." I teared up, embarrassed of myself. "First of all, don't feel embarrassed at all. This is why we're here, to talk about this tough stuff. No one should EVER yell in your face. EVER! Not even your kids. You have every right to stop that behavior the minute it happens." She said firmly. Sharon asked me how it makes me feel these reactions aimed at me, then asked for a rank the feeling on a scale of 0 to 10, 10 being the most enraged, 0 being not triggered at all. She later asked Jackie separate triggers. Then together we released our triggers. Sitting in our single chairs, Sharon told us to close our eyes, place your hand on your heart and she said things like, "I would like to love and accept myself regardless of having this issue." Then she slowly had us touch a specific part of our face, neck, or torso and release the emotion. Just as my healings taught me, emotions and triggers are meant to be released. Experienced, but then released. It's ok to feel feelings and emotions, but not to hold on and allow them to live inside you. The releases were like a cleansing, a clearing, a way to help NOT react towards our kids, who needed us to be consistent and solid, NOT on edge or furious. It helped me tremendously.

After only two sessions with Sharon, Jackie was in tears. "I don't see anything changing about Alison. I don't have much faith that things will get better for us to communicate about our kids. We just can't communicate. When we do, she just does what she wants anyway." Sharon was excellent at not letting us bash on each other. "Let's talk more about how it makes you feel when you communicate poorly."

"She just….." Jackie began to say, but Sharon cut her off and corrected her with, "How does it feel for you?" We discussed our reactions to each other, our struggles, but Jackie quit after three sessions. "Quite frankly, I can't afford it!" she said. But I kept seeing Sharon for therapy releases. I wanted to be a good mom for my kids. Sharon helped me define and enforce my boundaries with my kids and

I learned to say no to my kids when necessary. Gradually, like air out of a tire, the pressure released, the tension disintegrated. There's always a layer of emotions present. Releasing different layers of fear and anger through EFT calmed me enough to parent in a grounded, calmer way, without triggers.

Sharon advised reading "How to raise an adult" and other parenting books that encourage independent but not privileged children. She offered online voice presentations that I listened to for parenting. Before kids, I read lots of books, but until I lived with them and developed a true relationship with them, I wasn't sure how to love them or how to act around them. I thought it was only about discipline. But Reiki and the energy medicine taught me to open my heart to my kids, to listen to them. I learned to give and receive energy with them. They were dying for my attention and some independence in their choices. Over time, there were signs of relaxation at my house that I hadn't seen in my kids before. Maria put up posters on her walls, she wasn't allowed to do that at Jackie's. She set her own alarm clock. Jackie won't let Maria get up too early. Noah played in his room lying on his bed, drawing with his art box at his side. He couldn't take any art in his bedroom at Jackie's, it was only at his desk. They helped themselves to snacks anytime of the day, but at Jackie's they were only allowed after dinner, one snack. They bounced on the couch and the chairs, which they weren't allowed at Jackie's. They asked me more questions than ever before. We talked a lot more, listening and validating their ideas and opinions. They were less stressed about knocking over drinks, less stressed about spending money, less stressed. Whenever I overheard them quietly singing or laughing by themselves, it was a sign to me, they were relaxed and happy in our home.

My former household seemed to be built on stress and drama. One day, Jackie dropped the kids off at my house and Noah had two black eyes. "What happened?" I asked.

"Well," Noah said angrily, "I jumped off the counter for Mama to catch me and she didn't catch me! She let me drop to the floor!! So I banged my nose!" He looked at me for validation.

I put my hand on my mouth. I was scared for Noah and Maria. I couldn't believe Jackie wouldn't have instinctively caught Noah. When I confronted her, she said, "He lunged at me from a standing position on the counter, so I turned away to protect myself and he fell down to the floor and bumped his nose." I left it alone. I waited to see if anything else happened. Plus I wasn't there. How could I know the circumstances?

Another day, Noah was flipping out at my house, long tantrums, lots of anger, so I texted Jackie saying, "Has he been acting up lately? He seems to really be losing his temper today. Has he been having tantrums lately?"

Jackie immediately texted back, "I'm sorry to have to say this to you. Noah never acts like that with me." *Ah, yes*, I thought, *I can't co-parent with this woman. No way.* He lost his temper with her, yet here she was, insinuating that he only had tantrums with me. She blamed me, indirectly. Why did I even try to share information with her? I stopped texting her. Validation had to come from myself.

One Thursday evening, I cooked my grandmother's chicken soup for dinner. I was excited it turned out tasting so good. I happily placed the bowl down in front of my daughter. Usually, Maria didn't like anything I cooked and it hurt my feelings. As I went back to the kitchen to ladle out more, Maria started making groaning noises. "What!?! What is this???!!" She felt a bone in her mouth as she ate. She immediately flung herself off her chair onto the floor and rolled from side to side. Arms folded, leaning back on the counter, I watched her from the kitchen calmly, as she cried, "Oh no, not me! Oh God, I got a bone in my soup! Not me, not now! Oh my God!!! Oh no, not me! Why me!!?!?!" All of this seemed mildly amusing to me as I watched, but I withheld my laughter. I walked over to her and squatted down and gently rubbed her back, which was hot and sweaty from her huge feelings. "I'm sorry that happened to you. I'm sorry you got a bone in your soup." I said in a normal tone. She stood up, wiped her cheeks with the back of her hands, and went to her room quietly. To me, that was a win. I didn't stuff her feelings and neither of us attacked each other. I stayed grounded and apologized for it happening.

It took time, but my relationship with my kids thrived after I had my own peaceful space to share with them in the rental house. I became more self-assured, more capable. Regardless of the rules or the old ways, I slowly began to feel love inside my home, inside myself. It was an energy, an emotion, a powerful healing tool for my family. In the past, I thought I wasn't "good enough" to have kids. I assumed I was not "good enough" to be a Mom. I thought I used foul language too often. I didn't feel intelligent enough to parent. I was dark, grumpy, and pinched off socially. I was too judgmental. I didn't like rules or telling people what to do. I was incapable of parenting. Not loveable at the core, deep inside. Could I be a good parent after all? Part of me was still hiding. Maybe I could see value in myself, the light, then so would my kids. Maybe my kids helped me see the good in me. After much practice being with my children, and releasing guilt with Sharon, and creating new boundaries, I finally built up my sense of SELF as a Mom. My beliefs mattered as much as theirs did. I needed to see the good within, the kindness inside of me. With self-growth, I stopped being treated badly. I released the belief that I should give up my comfort for everyone else's. All of us could simultaneously be equals, treated fairly, treated with love, or least lessen the struggle for power. Compromise was possible. Maria said once, "Before, you were a cold Ma, but after you learned Reiki, you became a warm Ma!" Warm thoughts of loving my kids "as is" melted my cold, fearful heart.

Safe

Safe means something is not likely
to be harmed or lost.

"Why are you going this way?" I yelled loudly, with a tone of
'STOP!', as Erin merged the wrong way onto 84 eastbound. We were
east of Hartford, out to dinner with friends, and we needed to get back
west toward the city. My heart sank as the traffic halted to a complete
stop. There must have been an accident up ahead. We were parked
between two tractor-trailers. As Erin leaned past the steering wheel
and laid her head on my thigh in surrender, I massaged her neck.
Suddenly, I was glad to be stuck in traffic, because I was with her. We
had been friends for many years. Now we had been dating for several
weeks, and in that very brief time, she had already shown me her
thoughtful, kind ways by listening intently to my thoughts and
remembering my utterances. Her brave and playful style restored my
faith in having a successful relationship. Even when we disagreed, we
remained respectful of our differences. Conversations were laidback,
and we laughed long and deep, from the heart. She often said to me,
"You deserve to be happy. You are a beautiful conduit of pure love."
Even today, in traffic, she offered sincerely, "Ugh, I'm so sorry I went

the wrong way...."

"It's okay. Not much we can do now," I said, putting my hand gently on her back.

No one got angry. No one blamed. No stress. It was starkly different to experience life away from Jackie's abuse. For 45 minutes, we were stuck in traffic, and it was around 11 pm. We talked calmly to pass the time. It was freezing cold and icy, really icy. The radio reported the accident ahead was from a car crash that required some water to stop the fire, but it was so cold the water turned to ice on the road and needed time to thaw. They closed the highway. We were finally beginning to move out of traffic when the phone rang. I glanced down to see who was calling,

"It's Jackie," I said. "Why would she be calling me so late in the evening?"

Erin responded, "There's only one way to find out. Answer it." So I did. "Hello?"

"Are you in the area?" she blurted. Her voice was frantic. Noah was crying in the background.

"No," I said. "I'm stuck in traffic in Connecticut."

"Okay," she said. "You're no help to me, then. Noah is choking! We're in an ambulance, headed to the ER!" She hung up. My head went tingly and numb, faint, dizzy. Thank God we were out of the traffic, or I would have started running on foot. 'You're no help to me' kept echoing in my mind.

I tried to breathe and stay calm about Noah. I sent energy to connect with him in my mind. I sensed he was OK, so I comforted myself with that intuition. I had heard him crying over the phone, which meant he was conscious and breathing and alive. I believed he was safe, and that Jackie was an over-reactor.

I dropped Erin at home in Connecticut, then headed north to the Emergency Room in Massachusetts. Something made me stay calm, calmer than usual. Cars were in the ditches everywhere on the way north. Guilt settled like a close friend. Why wasn't I there for him? What if something happens to him? He's only four. What if I tried to stop the guilt of leaving my family from eating me alive. The self-doubting part of me kept saying, 'See! See! See! Your son needed you, and you were gallivanting with your damn friends!' The voice was not so different from Jackie's.

As I raced north, I texted Jackie for updates on Noah's status. They were brief texts like, "Where's Maria?"

"At our neighbor Helen's."

"Is she okay?"

"She was terrified. I had to wake her out of deep sleep and slip her into the police car until Helen picked her up".

My hands were tight and strangled the steering wheel. More guilt for not being there for Maria! As I drove, the weather was getting colder, it started to drizzle, but the roads were salted well in case of more ice. Still, to the right of me were cars that had slipped into a ditch, and many others were stopping on the highway. Usually, I hated icy roads and wouldn't even drive in snow, but now, my only goal was to get to Noah.

I turned in to the ER lot around midnight. I stayed in the car and took several deep breaths and cried a little to release the stress of getting there. When I entered the ER, no one was at the counter. I stood alone in the dim waiting room. Where could he be? Where is the staff? I wanted to search the halls for my baby boy. Eventually, a nurse walked me back to see him, then pulled back a curtain to reveal Noah and Jackie sitting in a cubical. He had pink cheeks but looked tired.

"Ma!!! They gave me popsicles!" he said all croupy sounding. He was bouncing on the hospital bed with Jackie in a chair next to him. I hugged Noah and ignored Jackie. I looked down at the ground when I entered through the curtain.

Noah told me more, "The ambulance brought me here! It was so cool!" I listened to him talking and bouncing, then asked, "How long do you have to stay here? What did they say?" I said the questions without looking at her.

"They said he might get out in about 4 to 5 more hours." Jackie updated me. "He needed meds to help him clear his airway," she reported.

I didn't know where to look or how to stand in the small space. I moved, so the bed was between us.

"Why?" I asked, "What happened?"

Defensive, she said, "Nothing happened. Noah kept throwing up and couldn't breathe in between bouts of puking!"

Noah chimed in, "I just kept throwing up, nonstop!"

"Well, I'm glad you got some help!" I leaned my forehead against his. He looked drained, but OK otherwise.

I sat on the bed, in the small, cramped room and hugged Noah. Jackie and I both focused on him. There were moments of silence. It's hard to flow with love toward your child in the same room with the person you distrust. I left after visiting for only a half hour. I hated being around her. Exhaustion and relief filled me after seeing

Noah safe. "I'll come back and pick you guys up later, OK," I said to Noah.

"OK, I love you Ma! I'll see you in a few hours!" he chimed back at me.

I didn't want to leave Noah, but I had to get out of that room. Jackie made me feel gross. She was a threat with her nonchalant attitude. Fake. Hospitals are creepy to me, but she was confident in an ER. Being a Nurse Practitioner, she used to work in a Pediatric Intensive Care Unit. It was her domain. She loved being there, and I hated it.

Before I left, Jackie asked if he could get discharged, but the nurses said: "No, not yet, there's no doctor around yet to discharge him." So I carefully slipped away. Now the wipers revealed that the drizzle was freezing on the windshield. Why couldn't it warm up a bit more than 25 degrees? It took a good 45 minutes to stay as slow as 30 mph or less on the drive. I could feel my tires slipping on the highway. My heart was pounding, my grip fastened tight on the steering wheel. When I finally got home, I was so happy to be safe; taking off my shoes, pushing my toes against the heels to peel out, throwing my keys on the counter, and exhaling. I kept the lights off, collapsed on the bed face first, and fell asleep for only an hour, and the phone rang.

"OK, come get us. He's getting discharged." Jackie said casually. She was looking forward to going home.

"What?" I squawked. "I just left there! I should have waited for the damn doctor instead of driving north!!! Ugh!!!" I said OK and agreed to get them, then hung up. Why did I offer to pick them up? Why didn't I stay there longer? I screwed up! I assumed since Jackie said it would be 4 or 5 hours until he got discharged, that it would be 4

235

or 5 hours, not 2. So now, I figured I had to get them…after all, it had been a long night for them too. They were sitting in an ambulance and a hospital bed all night.

But then I slowed down. Something invisible stopped me. I sat in the dark garage, in my car with my head against the steering wheel, considering all my options. Everything I learned these past two healing years was about counting me into all equations, all decisions. Using my voice, listening to my intuition, I hit the garage door button to open it. "It's not safe," I heard myself say out loud. I stepped out of the car and walked outside to slide two feet down the slope of the driveway like a surfer, arms out at my sides. It was solid ice, the whole driveway. I looked left and checked my road; it was dark and misty. I saw glowing red tail lights of one lone car fish-tailing, pressing their brakes. It was foggy, dense, sooooo cold, colder than it was earlier when the drizzle was freezing on my windshield. "No way," I whispered. "No way am I was driving when it's this icy, and I'm exhausted beyond tired." Holding my breath, I texted Jackie, because I was too chicken to call her to say "No" over the phone. "It's not safe to drive yet." I texted her. I was soooo scared to say "No" to anyone, but especially Jackie. It meant a barrage of feelings was coming at me. I braced myself for the worst reaction. She dialed me quick as lightning. My phone rang loudly.

I meekly answered "Hello?"

"You're not coming?!!??????" shot through the air.

"No," I said timidly, "it's too icy to drive now. I'll come later after it melts more." The lump in my throat was swelling and dry.

"Are you kidding me??!!!???? You're going to leave your son to roam the streets of Springfield alone in the middle of the night??!!!??" She was incredibly pissed. "You said you were going to come get us!!!!! And now you aren't??!!!??"

My heart ached, but I stayed consistent, "No," I repeated calmly.

She yelled more, "I should have known I couldn't count on you!! I should have known you would leave us here!! I shouldn't count on you EVER!! I gotta go!!! Noah NEEDS me!!!" She hung up on me.

She used those words several times in our nineteen years together, something about this night made me more aware of her, what she said and how she said it. I became more present. The negative feelings about myself had indeed clouded my vision of how thoughtless she was and how I shouldn't stand for it, and how bullying is cruel and unnecessary. No one should ever talk to me like that. It's never OK under any circumstances for anyone to verbally abuse me.

Relief washed over me, as did guilt, but I inhaled my breath then let it all go. This was one of the first times I listened to myself despite her. I stood up to her. I said no over and over again to save all of us from a potential car accident. I stood behind my Self for support. Three minutes later, she texted me saying the ER would let them stay there a while. The waiting room was safer than the roads. If someone else, like the ER staff, told Jackie it wasn't safe, it was valid, but if it was me, she labeled me "nervous and anxious." That's how she never hears me. I've no voice with her.

Going back to bed felt like a victory for me. I started whistling a tune as I walked back to my bedroom. My shoulders were loose and lower, my skin tingly, my heart full. It was the first break in my habit of putting Jackie before myself. I changed. Not only did I not sacrifice my safety for her, but I didn't try to explain myself to her, nor blame her for my decisions. I was neither the victim nor the aggressor, just me. I slept so very soundly for a few hours.

In the morning, around 7 am, I picked them up. It was warmer, no more ice on the roads. I proudly hopped in the car, fearless, and drove south on 91 again to the Bay State ER. Neither of us mentioned the conversation. The ER let them stay in the waiting room, on the couches for those few hours. Jackie acted as if nothing happened. Noah was smiling and still bouncy. He was happy to see me. She was pleasant and laughing now too. Wow. She had the nerve to tell me off and then casually accept my ride by morning with no mention of it, and no apology.

Words matter. Behaviors matter. At that moment, I held on to feeling grateful we were all safe. I was grateful to be free, to have a new way of being, to walk a different path, my way. No resentment, no regrets, less anger, and loads of love. Through the windshield, I smiled and squinted at the light, as the bright sun came out on that ride home.

Twin Shells

Twins are matching,
complementary, or closely connected.

Several months after the ice storm, I was meditating in Connecticut when I got the idea to create some closure on Noah's womb siblings. I write a letter to Noah's brothers. I walked out to the river bank, where I soaked in the sound of rushing water. Meditative bubbles formed from fast flowing water. I brought with me two candles and lit them in the grass on some rocks, one for each boy. The sky was blue with big, gray clouds. Gratefulness climbed up my chest. Erin was by my side, as I read the letter to the universe, to the brook, for Noah, for my family, for myself. "Thank you for setting me free. Thank you for teaching me forgiveness and the ultimate sacrifice. You gave your life for Noah and me, for Maria too, and Jackie. And thank you to Jackie for journeying with me in this part of my life. We don't always understand our life lessons, but we can be grateful." My heart burst as I read. There was a familiar pang of expanding in my chest. The ritual marked the end of that specific segment of my life. Then I blew out the two candles through my tears. I tossed two twin shells from York beach into the moving brook, to symbolize letting the boys go, to release them from me. We walked back to Erin's house holding hands, feeling somewhat sad. I said thank you and goodbye to my unborn twins.

Balance

Balance is an even distribution of energy,
enabling someone or something to remain upright and steady.

In the end, I learned to trust and listen to my universal energy. It's called love, specifically self-love. I used to think true love was giving myself away to become someone else, to please my loved ones. Love was a strain, a depletion. But love is the opposite, love is visualizing loved ones connected with us in their best light, their highest vibration; it's energizing! Love is a verb. Healings helped me forgive and release anger and fear build up in my body over the years. Once I was open, I could see I was being treated poorly by the one person who was meant to be my support. My spouse was supposed to be someone who helped me. A person who listened and cared about all of us in the family. Raising kids together is not an easy task, but it is a necessary and rewarding life change. I expected to have more love my kids were born. All you need is love to make a family, to have support to survive, and empathy for stress. After I left Jackie, I began for the first time to allow myself to receive kindness, understanding, and love from me, and from Jade and Ingrid and Erin and Iva and most of all, from my kids.

Energy taught me more intentional ways to love myself. I steered towards trusting and listening to myself, my intuition, my beliefs, my opinion, my radar for navigating life, rather than relying on others to tell me what to do. Self-growth became my new past time. Shamanic work and Reiki had one constant message: Love thy self. Love thy self. Love thy self. Not by being self-absorbed, but by practicing good self-care and making decisions based on my basic needs. Fill your cup with love so that you can overflow onto others. I can't hold anyone else up if I'm sinking. One simple example was taking my kids to the park rather than to the skating rink because I enjoy the park more. The skating rink made me nervous. Another example was staying home rather than going to the mall. My kids sometimes nagged too much for me to buy stuff at the mall. I might have a horrible time. I stayed home and played games with them instead because it was more my speed. I changed my mindset from entirely doing what Jackie and the kids preferred to include myself in the decisions, rather than making myself so resentful. What activity could we all do? Since we were a family, we should include all of us, not just the kids, and not just Jackie.

Meditating daily, I ask the universe for guidance. I believe in the unseen world. And sometimes when I am too low or lost, I ask friends who have my best interest in mind for their support or what to do, like Jade or Erin. That's what I want my kids to do also. I want them to trust their intuition, to initially ask for guidance inside of themselves. I want them to slow down enough to hear their hearts. No one else knows you as you know yourself. So I learned to value my inner spirit, my loving soul, not only my ego, not my judge. I never liked the responsibility of having a voice and taking a stand on anything, even creating rules for raising my kids. But I found a place I fit in, a balance. A balance between the two extremes of not caring what anyone thinks versus making decisions entirely on what someone else thinks. I can't thrive in someone else's belief system. I learned to define, develop, and listen to my boundaries and needs. Rather than following the leader, or doing everything the opposite of Jackie, I needed to evaluate the kind of parent I wanted to be, the kind of person I wanted to be. Regardless of the haters and the doubters and the judges, I had to find my style and be able to stand in my power, to become Alison.

"Every time you don't follow your inner guidance, you feel a loss of energy, loss of power, a sense of spiritual deadness," said Shakti Gawain. She is a pioneer of personal growth. To anyone who is scared and doesn't know how to begin again, I say, we all struggle to change our lives. Ask the universe, as your inner guidance for help. Shaman, Gurus, Spiritual leaders, and Reiki Masters all guide us towards our intuition so we can connect and hear our deepest desires. We are complex, emotionally and energetically. But our spirit is what makes us unique and strong and valuable. Imagine if we turn our judgments into praise and our criticisms into compliments. Use your inspiration, don't waste it. Use your heart, don't guard it. Use your power, don't fear it. Be brave. Be yourself. Accept everything, exactly as it is.

In the summers, I drive my kids to visit my family. I'm sitting on the deck facing my mom. She has one hand in a cage and one hand holding her whiskey. She leans back and proudly watches my kids.

The cage is where her cat relaxes and gets fresh air. The cage sits on the picnic table where we used to eat our dinners. My mom won't let the cat outside to roam free. When I was a child, we had two cats and two dogs that were free to go anywhere at any time. This cat is curled up in a comfy round bed purring as my mom scratches her cheek. My dad is stoking a fire in a tall, adobe, chimenea where we are going to roast marshmallows. My parents, my siblings, and I love to be outside near a fire where we eventually star gaze at nightfall. We've been doing it for years. "I need to be under the sky," my mom always says, and I agree. Noah is talking with my brother, Kurt while Maria is talking with Rose, Kurt's wife. Kurt and Rose are sitting on a bench in front of the chimenea waiting to roast marshmallows. I play some polka music on the radio. As the sunlight gets dimmer, the music gets louder, Noah lures Rose to dance by putting her hand in his and wrapping his arm around her waist. She laughs and bounces with him to the music. Then my mom perks up to the song "Roll out the barrel" and tells my dad to dance with her. He promptly gets up, and they polka beautifully, both of them singing to the words as they bounce and dance on their deck. I am recording it all on my iPhone and blasting the tunes at the same time. Rose reaches over to my brother and gets him up to dance too. Just then, Noah sees my father remove his sweater. This cues Noah to take his shirt off to reveal his naked belly, twirling the shirt over his head like a lasso, he yells, "Let's get this party started!!!!" and we all laugh, howling. I watch Maria leaning over and not breathing with joy, staring at Rose. Happiness fills my belly and my heart, watching them all enjoy each other. Then my dad chuckles at Noah and says, "Where did we get him!!?!"

The energy opened my heart to myself and my kids. My most

important lesson was to love myself, so I can rejuvenate, then love others, to base all my decisions on love, not fear. And when it comes to writing good books, relating best to other people, even connecting with kids; show, don't tell. Show them the way to be. Love them well and often, beginning at home. You can't change people, but you can love them. You can only change yourself. Kids do what you model for them, not what you tell them to do. I didn't want my kids to be exactly like me. I wanted them to become their unique selves. In the end, I was guided and compelled to model how to use my voice, to show my story, to speak up and be heard, so they can too.

Epilogue: Let it flow

I'm proof that miracles exist. I jumped without a net, for the love of my kids. They both saved me from myself and my attacking thoughts. Unable to accomplish what seemed natural, such as parenting, I assumed I was odd, inept, or broken. What if I am all those negative things? The universe answered me with, "love yourself!" I've lived happily in this adorable rancher in the woods for four years. I'm divorced from Jackie for three years, separated for five. Change takes time, yet it's worth it! I risked everything to get unstuck! It's not always pretty or orderly, but I always keep changing. I'm proud that I can change! We only get one life and it's so incredibly valuable!

Recently, I found a book called "The Alchemist" then randomly opened to a page that said, "…attaining the philosopher's stone means that you have learned to act on the authority of your own spirit without relying on any other source of confirmation or justification. You can bear not knowing whether you are good or bad, right or wrong. You have taken <u>full possession of your human freedom</u>. To label this as "arbitrary" is in no way a put-down. It just means that your magical deeds speak completely for themselves. In defense of them, you offer neither good intentions nor good results (though you may in fact have both meant well and done well.) You don't defend your magic at all. You just do it." This is what I've been striving to attain, the philosopher's stone. I strive for full possession of my own personal human freedom.

Creating life change can be challenging. Leaving my safe, professional career has been very scary, but worth it. I earn my income tutoring and writing and healing. My former long commute plus 40 hours a week on a computer was part of my daily stress. It was hard to do the same thing day in and day out for 19 years. A different, more creative vocation was calling to me. Stress was pulling me away from my kids and myself, my dreams, my purpose, my love of life. That's why I left my salaried job. My co-workers think I'm insane for leaving. I don't think they knew how unhappy I was working there. My dream was to come out from hiding behind my computer screen and interact with more people, to offer my skills and energy in a more meaningful way. I am now.

Writing is not a traditional job, but writing is why I'm here, to observe my life, to write about my life, to show others another way. I hope to have peace and joy from now on. So, I prefer variety in my purpose, which is what I have now. I do several things for income, not just one. It's my life, I get to choose what I do.

Today I drive as little as 3 miles to meet my students for a few hours daily. At the local library, I tutor high school or junior high kids who are disabled, anxious, or too stressed to attend school. Each child teaches me how easy and important it is to connect one-on-one. My very first student was too anxious to go to school in 7th grade. I tutored him daily for almost a year. He talked to me about his dreams. Today in 8th grade, he's thriving and doesn't like to miss school ever. Recently, he joined the Ultimate Frisbee team and made two new friends. The love from his parents and his therapist, and hopefully my love and attention helped encourage him.

I wanted to grow closer to my kids by loving myself as much as they loved me. I wanted to get love back. I had to catch up with my kids. I was so fearful of relationships! This book grew from my experiences with my kids and energy healings that lifted my anger, my sadness, my negative emotions. That's worth more than gold to me.

Maria is a tender heart. Adaptable and strong-willed, she began public middle school two years ago in 5th grade. She made many new friends. It was her idea to stop homeschooling, with my blessing. "I want outta this Mama Bear Circle," she said to me. Today, she's enjoying her new freedoms. Her grades are good. She's liked by her teachers and peers. At our last parent-teacher conference, the three teachers that were there said, "Maria is very well like and is always kind and thoughtful to others. We wish she would participate more in class." She is dedicated to ballet, more than her grades. "I want to go to Juilliard!" she tells me. I'm happy she's thriving now. No more bed making or hair habits.

Noah, now 8, wants to be a stand-up comedian with a huge heart of love. There is much less hitting from Noah and less violent outbursts. I'm working currently to eliminate all signs of violence with him. Sharon helped me come up with a new strategy. When I lecture too much, Noah's signal to avoid a fight is to say "Ma, lecturing" rather than mocking me or making faces or antagonizing me. My job is to stop lecturing. In return, my signal is to say to Noah, "Noah, rude" to get him to stop being disrespectful. It's been working. The other day, I began to lecture him, and he said, "Ma, lecturing" and waited. I gave him one thumb up and stayed silent. It worked beautifully, fight avoided.

We are all singing and dancing more in our home together! I'm teaching Noah piano. Maria shows us her dance routines for ballet. Center stage is where both of them may enjoy their leisure activity or earn their living. I'll be pleased with anything they choose, as long as it's theirs.

I still get doubts; they inevitably show up. I get incredibly fearful or stuck at times. Parenting is still my biggest challenge. Maria and Noah fight me and push boundaries sometimes, but I stay calm more. And more importantly, I don't beat myself up or loathe myself as much as I used to when I make mistakes. Oh, I make mistakes, but, I take myself less seriously now. For example, I tell myself I need more money and more purpose to be happy or to be a good parent. Then I realize I'm pushing again, trying to steer. Surrendering takes practice daily. I view my chatter and label it as stress or worry and later thank it for trying to make my life better, then I watch it go, like watching a car pass by. I notice the belief or the emotion and don't attach to it. Sometimes I cry and worry about whether I'm a good Ma, but then I try to let go and not push myself. I'm always learning the cycle of acknowledging then let go.

For extra support, I see my Shaman and vent to my therapist to gain and reinforce guidance. My kids trust me more now. Talking closer, listening, being present when they share thoughts, and resting my hand on them, shows them I love them. I read to them. I share myself with them, with my writing. They know I have other interests besides parenting. I am much more valuable to them as an example than any entertainment or material objects like Netflix or iPhones. "People come first, not stuff." Showing them, we all need idle time, downtime, daydreaming time off screens and unplugged; it helps us all be more creative and flowing. They see me enjoying writing, painting, drawing and playing guitar. It's what I want for them, more enjoyment, pretending, and dancing.

My Aunt Celia and I share and read spiritual books together. She is my godmother. She is the one who read me The Velveteen Rabbit all those years ago, telling us to be ourselves and embrace both the good and bad pieces of ourselves. We both struggle with other people's judgments day to day, but that's normal. The more we read spiritual books, the more we heal ourselves. Walking through life with her is a blessing because she reciprocates love so well, giving and taking, offering and receiving. We have a very special connection.

In the summer, I take time alone to vacation with my parents and my brother's family and my sister's family. About a dozen of us or more for 5 to 7 days stay in Sag Harbor, Long Island, where my grandparents vacationed, and their parents before them. My most loving relationships are with my parents and my sister and my brother. I laugh with them a lot. My connection with my family fills me with love. Talking alone with my brother or my sister is so special, even now. In fact, my one on one time with most of my family and relatives fulfills me. It took time for me to get good at being genuinely open and listening, but I enjoy hearing from each of them, daughter, son, mom, dad, brother, sister, in-laws, nephews, nieces. I don't care what they wear. I do care what's in their hearts. Once a year, I get my guitar out and sing and laugh by the Bay with my family.

Where ever I am, I write and meditate to start my day. Writing serves me, as a therapy, but also as an inspiration and a guide. I get answers in writing and meditation. My friendships are few, but the ones I have are strong and solid. I pray I get to make new friends and meet all of you who read and enjoy and gain something from these stories of my life.

My most significant personal change is that I trust energy more now. I rely on it to help me open my heart and flow. I call on it for help. Erin and I open our hearts daily to the universal energy. We study it and create a personal space in our daily lives to connect to energy larger than us, an energy that created the universe. Because of my relationship with my kids and Erin, I am learning to love fuller and deeper than I could have alone and isolated. Relationships are vital.

I don't pretend to know everything. But I surrender and give up steering when I feel lost or confused. I ask the universe to take care of the things I can't because my mind misleads me. I ask for help by praying. I read Rumi's poems daily. He always teaches me to flow towards Source. I read a 12-step book in the mornings. The consistency in all the teachings I've learned astounds me. I asked to be shown to live life with love, and I received many answers and methods. The theme is simple; acknowledge and let go. Our egos tell us false truths. Our minds chatter with fear and worry. Still, the practice of love is simple; acknowledge and let go of the ego, step aside to allow a higher energy vibration lead me.

There are the many methods that tell the same theme. Sharon teaches me to touch each meridian and then love and accept my emotions and my issues, then let them go. Iva teaches me to meditate, move energy, open to energy, and then flow. The 12-step program instructs me to "drop rocks" or to let go of the negative stories in my head. "Let go and let God." Eckert Tolle teaches me to live in the now to be more self-aware to quiet the ego. Byron Katie teaches me to write down my complaints about other people, then turn it around and apply that complaint to myself. Leo Buscaglia teaches me to fill my body with love and pass it on, overflow. Julie Cameron teaches me to write down every thought in my head in my morning pages journal, to flow and be creative, to keep the energy channel open. Reiki and Ingrid teach me to let go of anger and worry daily, then pull Reiki energy through your body. Shamanism teaches me to acknowledge the emotions and thoughts so they can flow out and not get stuck in my soul. Michael A. Singer teaches me to let go by sitting back in the seat of consciousness and observing my emotions and thoughts, then let them go. Do you see the trend? Flowing and letting go and surrendering are the major important methods towards happiness because our lower minds fill with negative chatter and false beliefs. I often need to remind myself of all of my above tools. Life is a gift. Accepting life on life's terms can be very challenging, but very beautiful!

I enjoy reading other people's stories. There is proof that Love is everywhere if we only acknowledge it, honor it, prioritize it, and appreciate it. Reiki is Love. Energy is Love. If you don't believe, then try it, try taking small steps to ask for help, or wish for change, or find positive ideas to come to you. There's always an answer, but you have to be open to it, and listen. Most of all, I need to flow, so I'm not pinched off and judging and closed up.

Traveling and connecting with others is my future hope. I took a plane for the first time at age 42. I used to be afraid. Now, I'm

47, and I'm flying! I wish to brave this Earth with my book in hand, and my love by my side, and my kids too if they want to travel. Globe-trotting! Book tours! I pray for courage and love to help me get through my time on this planet and witness love and spread love for many years to come.

As for Jackie, we don't speak. We text or send emails to communicate about our kids. But we both do our best not to argue because we love our kids fiercely. It's helpful that both kids have two parents, two opposing opinions, two different ways of doing things, and two sets of open arms for hugs. We try to be kind and contain our criticisms towards each other. There are lots of the same arguments repeating, but much less often. After all, actions speak louder and more transparent than words. I try to show, not tell.

Acknowledgments

I would like to thank all the brave people who had the courage to stand up and be heard against oppression. Thank you to all the people who felt fear in their body, yet kept stepping forward and creating a path for the rest of us. Thanks to my family and relatives, for being brave, rising to the many challenges life brought you. I'm grateful to my kids for coloring my life beautifully, teaching me how to love well, and for loving me unconditionally. Thank you to my mentors, coaches, and teachers who shared their experiences and their truth with me. I would like to offer many thanks to Melanie Bishop for teaching me to write relatable, detailed stories. Annie Tucker, I offer many thanks for all your gentle advice. Thank you to my love. Thank God you believe in me and my writing. I couldn't have crossed the bridge to you if I hadn't loved myself first. Here's to loving daily and living our dreams together!

About the Author

Alison was born and raised in a beautiful stone house, deep in the woods of Pennsylvania, where her childhood imagination ran wild and free. She enjoyed many team sports and friends. Taming her wild meant tamping her energy down. Anxious and shy, she avoided connections. To conquer panic attacks and navigate life, she began to study the human psyche, gaining her Master's degree in Sport Psychology. Her knowledge of biostatistics and clinical research enriched her career on many levels, allowing her twenty years of clinical and professional experiences in healthcare and medicine. She stumbled into several friends practicing energy medicine and sought counsel, healing, and self-growth. After lots of practice, she began to open her heart to others during her Reiki Master/Teacher certification in 2012. Learning to raise her two young kids prodded her to grow and gain spiritual strength and self-esteem which inspired poetry, creative nonfiction, and life stories. She now lives in New England where she tutors dissertation writing as well as junior high and high school students who struggle with anxiety or depression. She spends her free time in nature, writing, playing guitar, and enjoying her kids. Her life goal is to write more stories, give inspiring workshops, and awaken every person to the power of Love!